D0039310

The eagle is the winged lord of the upperworld, while the post it sits upon is the world tree which connects the lower-, middle- and upperworlds. The snake, symbol of both primal nature and the kundalini energy, spirals up the central *axis mundi* to join the opposites in a union of Wholeness — the perfect logo for Archetype Design.

ARCHETYPE DESIGN
House as a Vehicle for Spirit

By Vishu Magee

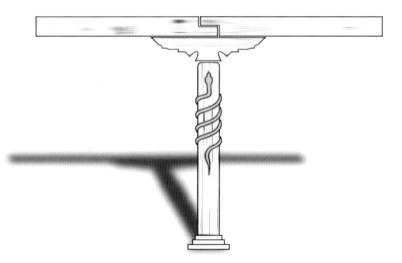

Published by Archetype Design Publications, Taos, New Mexico

Ordering information:
Archetype Design Publications
P.O. Box 2049, Taos, NM 87571
FAX 505.751.0038

For information regarding workshops or design services:
Vishu Magee
Archetype Design
P.O. Box 2049 Taos, NM 87571
e-mail: vishu@archetype-design.com
website: archetype-design.com

The eaglewing corbel is available from Southwest Spiral Designs 505.758.4974

Cover, book design, and graphics by David R. Doyle
e-mail: taosdave@newmex.com

Library of Congress Catalog Card Number: 99-90459

ISBN 0-9672163-0-3

Printed in Canada on recycled paper.

CONTENTS

Acknowledgments:

Deepest gratitude to the many great architects, philosophers, mystics and shamans on whose foundations this work is built. May this volume contribute to the wholeness and happiness of all.

Special thanks to those whose particular help and encouragement made my project possible: Sam Gusman, Diane Haug, Tav Sparks, Jai Lakshman, Kailash Paine, Hal Ross, Lenore Laupheimer, Ariadne Green, Theodor Grossman, Chris Pieper, Louis Jaffe, Kitty Whitman, Joan Reddish, Paula Baker, Daniel Goleman, Jack Kornfield, Joseph Goldstein, Sharon Salzburg, Ram Dass and above all, Stan Grof. Thanks also to my many wonderful clients whose support and confidence has helped me make my way.

It has been my great pleasure to work with David Doyle on the design and graphics for this book, and to see the various images come alive with the inflection of his own vision.

Thanks to my mom, who did her best to teach me how to write.

And most of all, my thanks and love to my family: Nancy, Jake, Jed and Aaron. This is for you.

FORWARD

Modern consciousness research and thousands of sessions of experiential psychotherapy have provided convincing evidence that our everyday reality of physical events, thoughts and emotions is merely the most visible portion of much vaster dimensions of the human psyche. When, for brief moments, non-ordinary states of consciousness ("holotropic" states) allow us to break through the shell of ordinary ("hylotropic") perception, we gain access to an astounding range of experience and an expanded sense of self. This inner reality is indeed a landscape of symbols, for which only the language of image and emotion is an adequate expression. Thus, in the context of this book, it is doubly significant that participants in holotropic sessions frequently associate their experiences of transcendence with the sensation of "going home."

The holotropic experiences of which we speak are usually reserved for moments of intensive retreat, focused transpersonal journey, or spiritual emergency. But, however we might choose to take our journeys of self-exploration, we are still left with the daunting task of integrating them into our lives. Here we often stumble, for in the present cultural context we are only beginning to build bridges capable of conveying transpersonal vision into a narrower consensus reality which stubbornly resists the expansion of consciousness.

The intriguing phenomenon we call "house" can provide just such a bridge between holotropic and hylotropic reality. As this book so skillfully points out, the parallels between the structures of the psyche and the structures of house are as powerful as they are fundamental. This should come as no surprise, for home is indeed our second womb — it is the matrix within which the human psyche has evolved since the earliest days in the cave, and it continues even now to be the vessel for a lifetime's journey from cradle to grave. Moreover, home life provides the primary interface between the individual and family, community and environment. Therefore, as consciousness is transformed through inner journey, house and home can serve as an immediately available vehicle for realizing that vision.

Such an understanding of house is not without precedent in western psychology. In 1924 Otto Rank wrote of primitive dwellings made "in instinctive remembrance of the warm, protecting womb." Carl Jung came to his discovery of the collective unconscious through a dream of a house, and later in his autobiography he described the house he built with his own hands, the Tower, as "a symbol of psychic wholeness." More recently, John Weir Perry has noted a direct link between 5,000 year-old architectural forms in Mesopotamia and symbols arising as ordering principles in the psyches of his Bay Area patients.

Archetype Design thus takes its place in a respected continuum of thought — adding, however, important new elements in response to the global environmental crisis. Here the link between spirit and sustainability is convincingly explored. In proposing that our own healing and that of the environment are in fact one and the same, the author directs us to an architecture and a lifestyle which are at once a direct expression of universal principles of nature and of our own nature. Various methods of inducing non-ordinary states of consciousness provide the means of accessing archetypal sources of creativity and transformation, while a set of innovative techniques provides the means of bringing visionary experience into healing and sustainable architecture.

At the millennium, we are faced with very serious challenges of our own making. Though ancient spiritual teachings, cutting edge consciousness research and quantum physics all point unambiguously towards wholeness, we nevertheless continue to live a lifestyle which threatens the very biosphere of which we are a part. This is a gap which must be resolved if we are to survive, and to this end work such as Vishu Magee's is a most welcome and indeed, essential contribution.

Stanislav Grof, M.D.
author of *The Adventure of Self-Discovery* and *The Cosmic Game*
Mill Valley, California, March 1999

INTRODUCTION

The circle, symbol of wholeness, is differentiated by the division of four which represents the processes of Nature within and without us. Four seasons, four directions, four elements — these are universal organizing principles. They form a cross, which is the interplay of the horizontal dimension in which we live, and the vertical course of transformation. Above is daytime, light, life, and the conscious mind, opposed below by night, darkness, death, and the Unconscious. In this most fundamental cosmogram all phenomena are implied, developing in balance and harmony according to the ordered cycles of time and space.

Houses hold an enduring fascination for most of us: it is here that we lavish a degree of energy and affection seen in few other aspects of our lives. African villagers may devote hours to painting intricate colored-earth designs on their mud walls, while American suburbanites are busy sinking small fortunes into their interior décor. Both act from the same impulse: whether decorating, remodeling, or designing anew, people strive to make their homes as much as possible into their image of the "dream house."

What is this powerful impulse? How is it that some houses speak to us? How do some seem to embrace us with comfort, safety and intimacy...or inspire and uplift us...or heal us and bring us together as family and community? And why is it that some houses, however lavish or correctly designed, totally fail to move us?

Twenty-five years of combined design work and spiritual practice have convinced me that the heart and soul of a house are primarily created not through design techniques, but by infusing the design with an ineffable energy or essence attained by diving deeply into the innermost realms of spirit and creativity. I began to experience this early in my career when, seemingly by chance, I would enjoy those spontaneous and fleeting flashes of insight which resulted in my best work. Over the years, some of my houses have radiated a certain spirit which, though evident to all, cannot be explained by the material details alone. Of course I can describe the array of design elements and their relationship to one another — but I can't always describe how I arrived there, let alone what was the glue holding the design together and giving it power. This has indeed been a mystery, one which has stimulated in me a growing interest in not only penetrating the elusive realms from which spirit springs forth as architecture, but somehow mapping a way for all of us to gain more reliable access to them.

In my explorations I have been amazed to find timeless forms of architecture actually lying hidden in the psyche like undiscovered gems. No less powerful are energies and patterns of movement which, once experienced, can take unique and dynamic form through one's individual creativity. Indeed, the sources of creativity which we usually consider accessible only to geniuses are available to all of us, if only we know how to get there. Thus, Archetype Design began as a method to enable us to tap into the wellspring of the sacred, the archetypal, and the creative.

But there is another strong force shaping Archetype Design, which is the need to respond concretely and effectively to both the global environmental crisis and our own social dislocations. So while the overarching view of this work is a spiritual or holistic one, within it is an activist stance which takes architecture as its vehicle. This is far from an academic exercise – put another way, Archetype Design turns on the perennial question of how to make our actions and lifestyle congruent with our values and vision.

By now we are all too familiar with the picture of a fast-degrading global environment and a decaying social structure. These are the signal challenges of our day, and to heal them is indeed the mythic and heroic quest of our time, to which architecture has much to contribute. But we will not be able to alleviate these conditions until we heal ourselves of the inner conditions of fear, greed and ignorance which created the outward problems in the first place. Ours is a journey – a Sacred Journey – in which healing ourselves and healing the planet are the same work.

The last three decades have brought us an astounding array of innovations in architecture: solar heating and electricity, environmental and community planning, energy- and water-efficient products, renewable and non-toxic building materials, recycling, drip irrigation, co-housing, organic and xeriscapic gardening, and more. These innovations have truly placed sustainable living within our reach.

Yet it is amazing that after all these years, and despite the flashiness of the New Age, so few people care to use these technologies or to embrace the less consumerist lifestyle they offer. Fortunately much of this technology is now mandated. But I have been repeatedly encouraged by clients' intentions to build with sustainability in mind, only to watch in frustration as deeply entrenched habits erode sustainability features one by one.

Though we are well aware of the mess we are in and have easy access to appropriate technologies, there seems to be a sort of paralysis when it comes to actually making a change. This is because, despite all our aspirations to environmental and social awareness, we remain addicted. Put more simply, the conventional consumerist habits remain more powerful than our desire to become whole.

More information is not the solution: thus far, public debate, environmental programs in the schools, economic incentives, and an avalanche of books and articles have raised our awareness to a limited extent but have failed to bring about radical change. What is required is nothing less than a fundamental shift in consciousness – and this is precisely what Archetype Design seeks to create.

Archetype Design offers a method which can radically change how we design our homes and communities because it first changes how we view ourselves. This method goes far deeper than intellectual inquiry – as the name *archetype* implies, it approaches design in the context of our deepest personal and collective natures. Moreover, the critical learning is experiential, enabling us to sense ourselves as profoundly connected to a global human family, to an exquisite but fragile ecosystem, and to a rich personal and collective legacy of archetypal symbols, wisdom, and energies reaching us from our distant past. A fundamental shift in consciousness can indeed occur, and the result is design which is sustainable, deeply creative, and supportive of ongoing growth and healing.

The key word here is *experiential*. For example, it is one thing to give lip-service to the idea that we are interconnected with the earth and its creatures. But if we actually experience the self in a visceral or mystical way as including all other people and species, then it's likely that our thoughts and actions will reflect this new and profound vision. We might never be the same again. Such experiences — of global or cosmic unity, of belonging to the earth, of limitless openheartedness, of being part of a timeless and sacred continuum — are transformative events which lie at the core of Archetype Design.

To be effective, however, any such transformation must relate back to everyday realities. The most important example is relationships: houses are usually designed for two people, yet too often homebuilding destroys the very relationship which it is meant to nurture. Not realizing how deeply our houses relate to our selves, we are generally ill-prepared to deal with the explosive personal issues and archetypal energies which homebuilding stirs up. Here is where preliminary work yields benefits we can immediately appreciate: we can identify and defuse the personality blocks which otherwise might blow up relationships already stressed by homebuilding; we can learn to create a healing and unifying vision for ourselves and our home; we can place ourselves in an archetypal context, bringing ourselves into alignment with primal energies and forces which will unite us rather than separate us.

Expanding this focus, we can explore what it means for a family to grow and evolve together so that our shared space will best support both our individual and collective selves. And if we take our home situation as a microcosm and succeed with our family relationships, then we just might be prepared to develop the openness and cultural sensitivity required to bridge the truly huge gaps presented by ethnic, cultural and economic differences in our society.

Personal transformation is thus a prerequisite in this work, and actual architectural design follows. Here too, Archetype Design has a different emphasis: the focus is not on problem-solving or technique, but rather on opening up creative channels so that images and forms may spring from sources far deeper than those which design practice usually touches. While architectural training traditionally emphasizes *mastery*, this work focuses on *mystery*.

The core work, then, is best accomplished in workshop and retreat formats where a number of techniques serve to create transformative experiences. Why then, this book? Quite simply, the book is intended to introduce the theoretical aspects of Archetype Design to the culture in general, and more particularly to those who might care to independently pursue the transformative work of which we have spoken. These concepts will help reframe our view of ourselves and our homes, and in some cases the thought process may even trigger spontaneous insight similar to what can be experienced in workshops. There is also the question of supporting the work between clients and architects: homeowners or design professionals who have found their way to Archetype Design may find the book useful to bring their counterparts into the same vision and method.

Many of the topics we will visit have already been presented skillfully and in great depth by other authors: sacred geometry, mythology, the sense of place, *feng shui*, solar design, permaculture, deep ecology, and more. Like slices of a pie, they converge at a centerpoint which holographically contains both the parts and the whole. The question is: how can we ourselves grasp that centerpoint? Archetype Design provides a core method to let us merge with the centerpoint, to weave the parts into an integrated whole — and moreover, to do so through our own individual and unique creative process so that the resulting design expresses *our* vision and *our* dreams. In so doing we can generate the kind of energy and magic which we all want to feel in our dream house.

What are the concrete results of Archetype Design for homebuilders, designers and architects? Buildings are likely to be environmentally friendly, non-toxic, solar, thermally efficient. They will include a sanctuary or sacred space. There will be a delicate interplay between the energies of Mother Earth and Father Sky, and a dynamism between our needs for solitude, intimacy and community. There will be a strong sense of comfort, of soulfulness, and of healing. There will be a high level of beauty and creativity, yet houses will be fundamentally simpler. For some, architectural forms might spring directly from inner visions or dreams; for others the images might appear gradually as the experiences of archetype, self, and connectedness slowly open into form.

If you are drawn to these results, then Archetype Design is for you. Along the way we will explore archetypal forms, both in nature and in our psyches. We will tour the global legacy of nature-based and sacred architecture. We will have experiences in meditation, mythology, dreamwork, art and ritual. We will practice relationship work and community building. Only at the end will we concern ourselves with floor plans and elevations. The work will be demanding — but the journey will be an adventure, and every effort will be well rewarded.

Long after our consciousness shapes a building, that building will return the favor by shaping our consciousness. So it's well worth performing the inner work which ultimately expresses itself in the design of house and home. This book offers several options for the creative journey, leaving the reader free to pursue whichever have the most appeal. Everyone will find some of these methods useful, a few of us will be drawn to them all — but any one of them is capable of taking us to the archetypal Source. While Archetype Design is most obviously relevant for owner-builders and design professionals, it is actually for anyone who simply loves home and wants to make it part of a life of spirit and sustainability. With that in mind, may we create living structures which will be a source of happiness and of healing for years to come.

PART ONE

MYSTERY

The sacred mountain stands as the mythological center
of the universe and the epitome of the Mystery – beyond
attainment, beyond comprehension, beyond mastery.

HOUSE AS A VEHICLE
FOR SPIRIT

Chapter One

Found everywhere in nature, from the sweep of the Milky Way to the movement of smoke, the spiral is the fundamental symbol of the Journey. Though it often feels as if we are moving in endless circles, actually it is not so, for at every turn we evolve to a new level of awareness to the extent that yesterday's lessons were well learned.

F ar more than most of us realize, when we design our house we design our selves. Certainly our home will shape our consciousness every moment we are there — and it will also condition our relationships, mold our attitude toward the community, and determine our place in the environment. This being so, we had better look deeply within and take care to design homes which can carry us far into the future in a healing and sustaining way. Thus the view of Archetype Design, to which we will return again and again as our primary point of reference, is this: *a house is a vehicle for spiritual growth.*

This is a much-needed departure from previous views. Almost anyone will agree, for example, that a house can tell a lot about its occupant. Past books have explored *house as a mirror of self*, detailing how homes reflect individuals' personalities, relationships, and upbringing. As far as it goes, house as mirror of self is perfectly accurate — but it stops at the level of psychology and remains a somewhat passive description of effects.

Our work is to take a leap to another level at which we become acutely aware of how *house both expresses and shapes our consciousness.* This is a far more dynamic and proactive attitude, and it alters both the goals and methods of house design. The goal, in short, is to design homes which are physically and emotionally healing and which bring us into a sacred relationship with the life around us. And the method, of course, is to begin that same healing now, and to develop that sacred relationship to life right now — in other words, to plant at the very beginning the seeds which will bring the results we want in the months and years to come.

Sacred Journey

In Archetype Design we speak simply of a journey towards wholeness — a sacred Journey to the Self. This journey is one of self-knowledge. On the one hand, it is a path of healing ourselves where we are fragmented and of reclaiming any of our lost aspects. On the other hand, it is a process of constantly expanding our sense of self until we arrive at a compassionate view of ourselves as including one and all.

There are good reasons for using the metaphor of The Journey. As we will see, myth has been embedded in mankind's buildings since the beginning, as for example when the spiritual journey is ritualized in the pilgrim's passage through thresholds or labyrinths on the way to the sanctum. In our work we, too, will be taking that mythic journey — except ours will be a journey to the Self within. Indeed, the parallels between the structures of the psyche and the structures we externalize in bricks and wood are a major theme of this book.

Our journey will be one of experiences, symbols, and metaphor. In this realm, images and emotion make more sense than words: *image-ination* is the appropriate language of both architecture and spiritual work. Thus to describe the journey with elaborate theories is not especially important: *what is important is that we actually take the journey.* For that, a clear intention and a minimal working knowledge of the path are all we need.

A functional description of spiritual practice begins by recognizing that we all possess the two basic tools of *awareness* and *intelligence.* These tools enable us to survive — but simply having them does not put us on the spiritual path. It is only when awareness and intelligence are combined in the process of *self-reflection* that we begin the essential spiritual work of inquiry and of self-discovery. Through self-reflection, for example, we begin to notice that thoughts and actions create results, and we see that we have a hand in creating the next experience by the choices we make in this moment.

It is amazingly simple: as we open to the fact that thoughts and actions create results, we naturally begin to make choices which favor less suffering and greater happiness. Our *intentions* gradually change as well. Though at first we may be concerned only with ourselves, we inevitably come to realize that any lasting happiness must include the happiness of all. Typically we begin by extending our concern to our loved ones, then perhaps to our community, and so on outwards. Thus the sense of self expands, and as our sense of interconnectedness grows we increasingly make choices which are in the interests of the whole. So our entire life becomes a process of deepening the experience of interconnectedness, allowing our sense of self to move beyond the narrow ego-mind in the direction of the One.

While the journey may at first be a tentative or part-time proposition, there may come a time when we desire to bring all parts of our life into alignment with the principles of non-harming, kindness and community. This is precisely where Archetype Design fits in, offering the tools to make our built environment part of the spiritual path.

We mentioned earlier that in house as a mirror of self, the building simply reflects the personality of the occupant. But in house as a vehicle for spirit, the building becomes a dynamic partner in self-reflection: we create the house, and the structure then shapes our consciousness. For example, we might craft a particularly light and airy room, intending for it to uplift us. Usually it will do just that — we shape the room, and it obligingly returns the favor. But what happens if it doesn't work? Suppose we find ourselves feeling dark and dense even in that bright room? Now, if we are aware enough, the contrast between our mood and the room has the potential to expose our gloominess, prompting us to consciously elevate our mood. So with a little effort, our mind becomes light and airy again. What occurred was an interactive process by which the house served to restore us to awareness and uplift the spirit.

Here it is important to distinguish between sacred space and house as a vehicle for spirit. *Sacred space* is a special building or room dedicated to a sacred function such as meditation or prayer. *House as a vehicle for spirit* acknowledges the entire house and all its functions as a dynamic element in the spiritual growth process. Whereas sacred space is reserved for moments of intense spiritual focus, house as vehicle for spirit recognizes that opportunities for awakening lie in each moment, and that how we live is just as important as how we believe. In this view, the bathroom may become a place of purification, the kitchen a place of healing, and the quality of mindfulness we bring to the moment is what invites transformation.

This all-inclusive view of spiritual practice is hardly new — indeed, many cultures, notably Japan, accord distinct ritual functions to the different parts of a house. However in our culture it is somewhat revolutionary to regard our homes this way. We tend to view our home as our castle — the ultimate physical and emotional refuge where we can indulge ourselves and where nobody can tell us what to do. So to some it may come as unwelcome news that here (*especially* here!) we have a wonderful opportunity to awaken. But this is the leap we must take, for the old saying holds true: it all starts at home.

Personal Transformation

In the conventional design situation the prospective homeowner starts with a budget, a building site, a wish list, and a set of images, styles and impressions which eventually get woven into a structure. Underlying these is a subtler set of values, habits, and beliefs which usually remain unarticulated but nevertheless become embedded in the house. This is precisely how a house becomes a mirror of self. But too often the process is an unconscious one, with the result that we build into our homes archaic attitudes and lifestyles which limit or imprison us later on. For example, an infantile need for security could cause us to build a home with small segmented spaces which would feel extremely confining if we later began to feel more secure and expansive. Similarly, a need to feel and appear successful might result in a house packed with showy amenities which could become unsatisfying and burdensome just a few years down the road. These are expensive mistakes of the sort we usually try to avoid.

There is a story of a woman who spent many thousands of dollars and endured months of stress to remodel her bathroom. It was the classic construction nightmare of everything gone wrong. Only when the job was finally completed did she realize that the room had never really needed remodeling — it was *she* who needed to remodel her relationships with men, but she hadn't been aware enough to see it at the time. She had to take the circuitous and costly route of working it out through her house — and it still didn't solve the real problem. The lesson, clearly, is to work out such problems in advance so that house design can express and create happiness and wholeness.

Since it is always true that beliefs and conditioning drive our decisions and actions, it follows that in design, too, the greatest potential for positive change lies in *preliminary* inner work. It is here, right at the outset, that we have the greatest opportunity to divest ourselves of excess baggage and set our sights on the highest goals. Thus the journey of Archetype Design begins with a process of intensive personal exploration and transformation. This is the experiential work offered in workshops and retreats, which of necessity goes far beyond the traditional scope of architectural study.

The first level of the work deals with familiar psychological territory as it relates to building. We begin by identifying issues which are in our conscious awareness, we evaluate them, and then we apply appropriate problem-solving techniques. This might include setting goals for a design project, identifying the material and financial parameters, and pinpointing unusual challenges or critical problems. When couples are designing together, we examine rather carefully what house signifies, how it can support both the individuals and the couple, and how the relationship can grow through the building process. Generally such work will also uncover emotional material which has been lurking *below* the level of awareness, and we respond by bringing that material into awareness and finding ways to creatively express and resolve those issues. For example, it's common for emotional needs connected with childhood experiences of home to lock us into rigid — and usually unconscious — notions of what a house should be. Our task is to identify and resolve those needs so that we won't have to build an entire house to satisfy them. In a similar way we consciously deal with the fear and anxiety which is typically associated with money and major decision-making. This is nitty-gritty, but extremely liberating work which is seldom addressed in architecture school. If done thoroughly, such psycho-emotional work greatly facilitates the deeper journeys ahead as well as the design process itself.

The next levels of transformation involve moving past the ego to dive deeply into the unconscious part of our psyche. For design purposes the principal goal is to tap the primordial wellsprings of creativity and inspiration — in other words, to draw from those visionary and creative sources which our culture usually reserves for mystics and artistic geniuses. In truth, as one will quickly see in the workshops, it is rather easy to access these realms through breathwork, dreaming, and inner journey techniques. And so, with practice, we reach the abode of the *archetypes* — the primordial forms and patterns of energy which provide the templates for all outward form. Here, for example, one can become immersed in dazzling mandala-like symbols encoded with the very ordering principles of nature. One may see pyramids and temples which are direct representations of sacred geometry. Or one might merge with the goddess Gaia, the embodiment of the entire biosphere and the inspiration for sustainability. These are the creative gems which we hope to bring back from our inner journeys.

Such journeys unfailingly satisfy the objective of transformation, which is creativity's twin. This is because in order to enter the transpersonal realm we have to temporarily suspend our usual sense of self, allowing it to dis-integrate. When the journey ends and we return to the everyday ego-mind, it is no surprise to find that it fits awkwardly: like a garment that is too small, the ego has to soften and stretch to the shape of a newly expanded sense of self. Thus we obtain a dual result: creative insight which applies to design as well as transformation into a greater human being.

At this juncture the reader should understand that the Journey, far from being some sort of amusing game, is a real adventure with real thrills and chills. For as we journey deep into ourselves we find dark regions as well as light, often swirling with immense, primal energies which can frighten as much as they inspire. Like the mythic heroes who encounter wrathful monsters, bewitching temptresses and seething maelstroms in the course of their quests, we ourselves must surmount numerous tests and challenges in order to reach our goal.

Most of us are only too eager to enjoy bliss-drenched experiences of creative inspiration — but how we respond to the dark side of ourselves is another matter entirely. A relevant example of the dark side is the consumerist addiction which we all carry to some degree: we, all of us, are caught in the ultimate destructiveness of consuming our very environment. Like junkies, we look to the next fix, unconsciously fleeing the gnawing terror of what might happen if the supply were to stop — and all the while we deny our addiction, telling ourselves that it's good for the economy and that technology will save the day. However, in Archetype Design we won't be able to get away with such denial. Sooner or later the journey will bring us face to face with our demons — perhaps *literally* so in the guise of archetypal monsters, or possibly as feelings of terror and emptiness, or as intense bodily pain. At such moments the only choice is to turn back or to continue the journey by fully opening to the fear and pain, allowing insight and healing to spontaneously arise, as they surely will. In time we learn that there is an inner intelligence at work, guiding us on the journey by presenting just those experiences which we need for our growth and which we are also capable of handling.

The full range of human experience is appropriate material for this quest, though at first glance much of it might not seem to have anything to do with architecture. The point is simply this: the more we know ourselves, the more we have healed ourselves, and the deeper we have journeyed into our creative potential, the better will be both our design results and our human being.

Designing for Change

People frequently people build their homes with the idea that, when the last nail is driven and the furniture is moved in, they'll at last have the dream house in which they can live happily ever after. This is the idealized home of movies and novels, which is so often an attempt to recreate childhood experiences of comfort and safety. But although we'd like to think that our home can be the one solid haven amidst the storms of life, such a myth flies in the face of reality. For change is constant, and life is simply moving too fast for us to know with certainty what our needs will be even a year from now.

In architecture, as in any other area, change is a central feature of life. Building and design technology is evolving faster than ever. Styles and trends cycle with amazing speed. Social and economic conditions, the environment, and even the climate to which we must shape our designs are constantly and rapidly changing.

No one wants to build a house which becomes outmoded within a decade. Neither do we want to be short-sighted and create a dwelling which we ourselves outgrow. Somehow, in our homes as in our lives, we must factor in the reality of change. This is particularly relevant in technical areas involving energy use, water conservation, telecommunication systems, transportation, and non-toxic materials. However, the change we are undergoing as human beings is actually *more* dramatic and urgent. Dramatic, because a wholesale shift from an ego-centric to a world-centric view is in process. Urgent, because neither we nor the earth as we know it will survive if positive and healing change does not come quickly. Our social structures and the shape of our relationships seem to be no less in flux. So our homes should both support and stimulate personal change. This notion — of house as change agent — is a revolutionary concept not found in the mainstream architectural curriculum. But if form is to follow function, then we must proceed from the understanding that change in the human being is a constant and necessary function, and one which building design should optimally support.

Is it possible to predict change? The answer, of course, is no. But we can probably agree that the desirable direction of change lies in the complementary needs of the global ecosystem and the human being. For the ecosystem to flourish, we must develop a holistic worldview and a sustainable lifestyle to support it. And for ourselves to flourish, we must expand our sense of self in the direction of interconnectedness and develop social structures to match. In fact, the needs of the planet and of humankind are the same.

Sustainable houses which express a sacred relationship with the earth are most likely to support our personal growth, because they are founded on the same timeless principles of nature which govern our journey and order all of life. These same principles dictate that, rather than design with only ourselves in mind, we must create and maintain a dynamic relationship with the environment and with community.

Community:
Our Collective Self

Neither the ecosystem nor the human race needs another New Age dogma which fails to yield concrete benefits in areas such as resource utilization, pollution control, biodiversity, and social harmony. House is a vehicle for spirit, and it is after all the nature of spirit to expand outwards and creatively express itself in action. Thus the emerging ethic of Deep Ecology is simple: we are separate from neither the planet nor the beings upon it, and we must work for the health and happiness of all.

When it comes to building design this is no idle sentiment, for the impact of the construction and subsequent use of a building is enormous. This impact is on our *collective* resources and environment, and it is further compounded at the level of *community*. Any advance towards sustainability which we make as individuals will contribute towards the collective well-being. Knowing this, many of us feel the call to contribute to a broader arena of ecological and social action once our own house is in order. Applying the principles of Archetype Design to community planning is a logical next step, for *no house has ever made complete sense except in the context of community.*

A first step in expanding the scope of work beyond residential design is to consider the potential of collective or community strategies. It is encouraging that minimization of environmental impact through high-density building and greenbelt preservation is already becoming standard planning procedure in many communities.

This is just a beginning: for those ready to let go of the 'traditional' nuclear family model of living separately, intentional communities offer tremendous benefits — materials and energy are saved, facilities such as workshops, gardens, studios and fitness centers are collectively available, and a support system is at hand for social needs such as child-, health- and elder care. Co-housing is another collective approach which is still relatively undeveloped. Though community living seems to run counter to our much-valued independence, there is no denying that the number of communities has soared in the last few decades, forming around themes including spiritual practice, ecology, retirement, and education. It may well be that the needs of aging baby boomers will be the occasion for major breakthroughs in our patterns of living over the next decades.

If service implies outreach, we might explore community approaches to the care of children, elders, the disabled and the homeless. Once again the key is interconnectedness: it is essential to include everyone in the circle of community rather than seek institutionalized solutions which further fragment society. Another key is to avoid imposing the dominant white cultural values on other ethnicities, but rather to draw out cultural and ethnic inflections and give them full expression.

Last, but perhaps most exciting, is the idea of taking appropriate technology to the underdeveloped countries whose ecosystems and resources are frequently in worse condition than ours. Whereas it has historically been difficult for westerners to bring cultural sensitivity to bear on such outreach, Archetype Design positively thrives on cultural diversity, offering a method for technology to be beautifully clothed in the forms and values of traditional cultures. Such efforts are essential, for on this small planet one country's loss of habitat and resources is everyone's loss.

ARCHITECTURE
AS BUILT MYTH

Chapter Two

Similar to the spiral, the labyrinth symbolizes the heroic journey into the unknown in quest of spiritual knowledge, transformation, or healing. The Unknown, the Underworld, the Unconscious – all are synonyms for the Mystery which must be penetrated before the Hero can return with the prize. The monsters, maelstorms and sirens he or she must conquer are none other than the inner demons of fear, ignorance and desire.

As far back as we can trace, builders have expressed their worldview through architecture. Worldwide, the primitive hut in the round emulated the horizon and the circular forms of nature. Black Elk of the Lakota Sioux stated:

> *"The circle helps us to remember Wakan-Tanka, who, like the circle, has no end. There is much power in the circle, as I have often said; the birds know this for they fly in a circle, and build their homes in the form of a circle; this the coyotes know also, for they live in round holes in the ground."*
>
> — J.E. Brown, *The Sacred Pipe*, p. 92.

Teepees, yurts and hogans were experienced as microcosmic, and the traditional or ritualized way of using such structures expressed a mythological way of living in harmony with the forces of earth, sky and the four directions.

The technology of man's early era no doubt placed constraints on what builders could do, even as it mirrored the degree to which those cultures lived in touch with the earth. As building technology evolved in pace with human consciousness, new architecture arose expressing new myths. Society became more complex and differentiated, so that by the time of the historical period the focus in architecture was on royal and sacred community buildings. Pyramids, ziggurats and stupas represented the world mountain or center of the world, around which ritual activity turned in emulation of the lawful order of nature. Centuries later the great medieval mosques and cathedrals encoded new myths of pilgrimage and surrender to a single Creator. In our era, a materialistic time with an emphasis on economic achievement, the skyscraper monolith has been both the altar of business life and the symbol of man's mastery of nature and his challenge to the skies.

To the degree that architecture is "built myth," we can benefit from understanding more about myth, how myth becomes encoded in a building, and in what way we are building myths even now.

A Brief History of Myth

Mythology is so vast and so full of insights that any brief treatment of it risks trivializing a subject worthy of a lifetime of study. Fortunately, the goal of this chapter is rather specific: to provide an initial point of contact with myth, and to simply open the door to this incredibly rich "treasurehouse" of wisdom by facilitating actual experience of it. Here, perhaps more than anywhere in this book, the reader would do well to visit other works on the subject

Myths began as stories by which primitive man attempted to both explain and reconcile himself to the inexplicable forces of nature. Death, for example, was a terrible and bloody fact of life for people whose survival depended on the hunt. Early man's response was to create myths and rituals of death-and-rebirth which ensured the return of the quarry as well as promising another life for the people. Thinking was at a magical level, and the shaman was the medicine man called upon to mediate between the small controllable world of the people and the much more vast, shadowy realm of the spirits. This was indeed a mysterious and mythic realm where animals, plants and places spoke to the humans through the shamans, and where man was just one part of a seamless flow of nature. Maintaining this animist connection to the natural world was critical for survival.

Jungian analyst John Perry describes the origins of myth in terms of a distinction between the secular and the sacred. The secular was the realm of the everyday events which man could more or less control. The sacred had its origin in those fearsome natural events which man could neither understand nor manipulate – they were charged with the emotion of terror, and man dealt with them by creating myths by which he could feel a sense of security in the midst of awe-inspiring forces. Uncontrollable weather, for example, was personified as deities which could be propitiated, while myths of death-and-rebirth arose in response to the central mystery of our own impending end. Myths had a dual aspect of *image and emotion* – compelling, down-to-earth, life-and-death emotion – and it was that emotion which energized the image and made it sacred. (Perry, *Lord of the Four Quarters* p. 24)

Of great significance is the fact that the earliest myths, dealing with primal themes such as creation, death-and-rebirth, and the forces of nature, are remarkably similar the world over. An example is the basic cosmology of Father Sky above, Mother Earth below, and the human realm in between. Another example of primitive myth is the Hero, in which a human journeys into the Underworld, braving temptations, monsters and death itself to bring back a lost soul, a symbolic object or an essential truth. Other important examples are the symbols to be found everywhere in dreams, art, and visions: circles, crosses, mountains, trees and snakes, to name a few. So ubiquitous are such motifs that they are considered to represent inherent and universal elements of the psyche. Jung named them *archetypes*. Such archetypal myths and symbols form the core of mythology, and they will figure again and again in our work.

As man's mastery and thinking evolved over many thousands of years, his world gradually shifted from the mythological and the sacred to the controllable and the secular. The myths changed, too, continuing to provide a template by which mankind could live. For example, in the era of the archaic kings of Mesopotamia (ca. 3,200 B.C.), hunter-gatherers had become farmers, complex societies had evolved, and astrology, mathematics and a written language were in use. Accordingly, the city-state was conceptualized as a microcosm of the lawful natural world, order in the realm was embodied in the sacred person of the king, and the cycle of the seed, the plant, and the four seasons replaced animal spirits as central sacred symbols. Architecturally, the ziggurat at the center of the city represented the world mountain and provided a symbolic and ritual ladder to the realm of the gods. From there the city extended out in four directions, bounded by the circular perimeter of the realm. This was the mythic worldview at the beginning of high civilization, precisely expressed in the architecture and ritual of the day.

But now we come upon an earth-shaking observation: five thousand years later, Perry observed the same images and patterns — of sacred kingship, of renewal rituals, of the quadrated circle — unfolding in the psychic presentations of his psychiatric patients! It is as if the restorative or ordering principles which informed the myth and architecture of archaic times had remained embedded in the unconscious, ready to serve us again even now:

> *"Here was a good possibility that the complex ritual in the seasonal festivals of archaic times was composed of the same elements as the reconstitutive process in the psyche, the one faithfully mirroring the other. I pursued the quest...and found that the further these explorations took me, the more clearly did the parallels emerge."*

– Perry, p.4

The evidence suggests a unique period of civilization when there was a one-to-one correspondence between architecture and certain universal ordering patterns in the psyche. So powerful was this architecture that in the ensuing centuries it diffused throughout the world, taking on the cultural inflection we can still witness at Giza, Palenque, or Taos Pueblo.

The dawn of the major Occidental religions saw among the Semitic peoples an unprecedented new myth of a single Creator god from whom man has been estranged and to whom he must reconcile himself. Gone was the ancient trust in an innate natural center which reflected the unified natural order of the world. The new myth divided the world between good and evil and reflected a view of revealed truth, of authorized religion and the splitting off, both socially and psychologically, of whatever views and energies were deemed pagan, satanic, or otherwise unacceptable. Architecture followed suit: the cathedral renders this cosmology by placing the sanctum above and apart from the aspirant and by portaying the battle between good and evil in the iconography of saints, angels, gargoyles and devils.

Until this time myth had reliably fulfilled what Joseph Campbell lists as its four essential functions: first, myth enabled man to cope with the reality of death; second, it provided a cohesive cosmology or worldview; third, it promoted the behavior necessary for the survival of the given society; fourth, it supported the psychological processes of maturation, aging, and dying. (Campbell, *The Mythic Dimension*, p.180) The process had worked beautifully for at least tens of thousands of years, with myth slowly evolving in pace with man's technology and ever-sharper thinking. But two historical trends more than any other have drastically altered the role of myth.

The first trend has been 2,500 years of humanism which began with the Greeks, flowered in the Renaissance, and has reached its climax in our own country of rugged individualists. The Greek poet-philosophers began it all with those tales of tragic flaws and of men defying the gods. Medieval bards, romantic novelists and modern existentialists made their successive marks, until by now it is largely left up to the *individual* to define his or her place in the universe. Whereas formerly the myths taught by shamans, priests and elders had provided social cohesion, myth-making has become much more of an *ad hoc* affair. And the results, as we see daily in the newspapers, have been decidedly mixed.

The second trend has been several centuries of rapid technological expansion and mastery over the environment. Copernicus and Galileo upset the applecart of Biblical myth, Descartes and Newton replaced it with a smoothly ticking Swatch, and modern capitalism has fueled the rush towards the bigger and the better. Today the secular has largely edged out the sacred, and the guiding cultural myth has become one of confidence in material gain and technological progress. Ours is an age of mastery over mystery. The old myths are inadequate for the times, and no contemporary culture is able to generate new myths in pace with ever-accelerating change.

Meanwhile it is clear that our mode of thinking, which has gone from magical to mythological to rational, is pushing against some sort of natural limit. It seems we've missed the point which those old Greeks knew so well when they wrote about hubris and described what happened to Icarus when he dared to fly too close to the sun. In our own minds (which is to say, in our own myth), our mastery of the environment is so complete that we have little fear of the uncontrollable. Our cultural myth of the technological fix provides a formidable defense against the very thought of losing control, and it blinds us to the effects of our contemporary hubris.

But clearly there are forces beyond our control — and if we don't fear them, then perhaps we should. Global warming, the vanishing ozone layer, environmentally caused disease, AIDS, gang violence, addiction, mental illness, nuclear threat, and degraded ecosystems are all here to tell us that we are in very serious trouble.

Creating the New Myth

While it is tempting to look back longingly to the good old days of mythology-driven culture, the simple fact is that ours is an age of individualism, of technological sophistication, and of rapid telecommunication-driven change. It is equally evident that our thinking mind has evolved into a prodigious tool. Nor are these trends likely to reverse themselves. So the challenge, of course, is to redirect these energies in a positive way.

At the same time it is also true that we humans embody all kinds of wisdom which is our legacy from the past. The entire course of evolution is phylogenetically encoded in our genes and in our DNA. We have an animal nature. We have the capacity to see reality magically. Archetypal energies teem in our psyches. We have an ancient sense of being one with the natural order.

And we certainly continue to think mythologically. Here again we would like to utilize all of these gifts in a positive way — but there is no going back to the magical or mythological mind of bygone ages, however romantic it might seem. Whatever ancient wisdom we embody was not equal to the challenges of the last 500 years and is certainly not capable of leading us into the future except in partnership with a new and higher awareness. This new awareness will be a transpersonal or spiritual one in which we authentically find our identity as an inseparable part of the whole of life.

To use a familiar metaphor, we could say that the thinking mind and technology are the tools, while ancient wisdom combined with higher awareness are properly the master. Establishing and regulating the correct relationship between these forces is historically the job of myth — but in our era we shall have to create such myth anew. A new myth will be unlike any before, because as author David Feinstein points out, this is the first time that consciousness, rather than events, is driving history. Democracy, prosperity and information have given great numbers of us the ability to self-reflect on events and act out of intention rather than from culturally determined responses. This is a very positive and promising situation as we go about creating new myth in a conscious way.

The new myth, though different insofar as it is consciously created, will *functionally* perform much as myth always has, because myth primarily operates *unconsciously*. Myth acts outside of awareness, even though it may have its origins in conscious experience. So there is a bit of hide-and-seek to myth — which, as every child knows, is very big fun. No sooner do we adopt a myth than it begins to direct our lives — so we had better be very careful to generate a myth which is wholesome, healing, and flexible. We should also be prepared to identify and release any outmoded myths which we might still be carrying. The shadow side of any myth is that it can amount to little more than superstition, masking ignorance behind the veneer of taboo and blind faith.

In investigating exactly what belief systems and templates are unconsciously guiding us, what we find is several levels of myth: *personal* myth is the collection of convictions we have formed individually through experience and through our own process of self-reflection; *cultural* myths are those we have assimilated from family and society; *archetypal* myths are expressions of patterns which inhere to biology and are fundamentally universal to mankind.

We gain access to the different levels in different ways. Cultural myths are identified through disciplines such as anthropology and psychology, but they can also be explored through guided imagery and ritual, which is a bit closer to the mark in terms of the language and metaphors of Archetype Design. We can work with personal myth in similar ways. Archetypal myth, however, is of another order entirely and must be teased out, primarily through dreams, transpersonal journey, art, and the study of mythology. This is where much of the experiential component of Archetype Design comes into play: meditation (to develop the primary tool of one-pointed awareness), transpersonal journey and dreamwork (to contact archetypal sources of myth), journals and small group work (to explore personal and cultural myth), and art and ritual (for integration, self-expression, and fun). From there it is but a short step to generate our own personal myth.

To jumpstart our creation of a new myth, let us return to the vision of the Sacred Journey. It could be described in a story such as this:

In a moment beyond time, and in a place which is everywhere, the earth teeters on the brink of destruction while the heroes (all of us) struggle valiantly to regain our lost connection with both Mother Nature and our own inner nature. There is no time to lose: delay means death. Along the journey to distant peaks we traverse dark places and encounter frightening demons and temptations (our own fears and desires). As we overcome them we gain the power to see landmarks which had been hidden from us, and to hear the inner guidance to which we had formerly been deaf. We make many stops to heal the earth of wounds left over from the long Dark Age. We begin to ascend the peaks. Though our power increases, we cannot complete the journey alone – we must join together in community and bring all the people along in step. At last we reach the mountaintop and its longsought sanctuary of Illumination, but to gain admittance we must make one last offering, which is to relinquish our dominion over the earth in favor of stewardship and unity with all.

Such a myth, or fable, is a simple way of linking the challenges of our day with the timeless Hero's quest of healing or enlightenment in service of the greater good. The supranormal energy and determination of the Hero are in fact within each of us — and judging from the versions of a new myth which are everywhere emerging in song, novels, dreams, and inner journeys, many of us are indeed beginning to hear the call to the Hero's journey.

Building the New Myth

For many decades our homes have reflected the dominant myth of the Industrial Age, which has become one of mastery and of material comfort such as the kings and queens of old could not imagine. Familiar aphorisms which express the old view of house include: "all the comforts of home," "a man's house is his castle," and "a woman's place is in the kitchen."

We are a material culture, and when we go about designing our houses we tend to focus on that which is material — so much so that many prospective homeowners find it difficult to approach design in any other way. We view the kitchen in terms of countertop tile, appliances, and modular cabinets. Bathrooms are described in terms of fixtures, faucets, tile, mirrors. Living rooms are made up of views, high ceilings, fireplaces, furnishings. And the entire project is determined by considerations of budget, resale value, and current style. The result is straight out of the American Dream, right down to two cars in the garage and mortgage payments to match.

How would houses be different if we were building the new myth of the Sacred Journey? Remembering that Archetype Design is *not* design-by-formula, a good start might be to ask these questions:

- What would happen if we regarded the kitchen as a place of healing?
- How might we design bathrooms if we viewed them as places of purification?
- What would bedrooms be like if they were intended to be sensuous and feminine places for dreaming and lovemaking?
- How can living and dining rooms serve to nurture family and community?
- How can children's areas encourage a playful and imaginative outlook on life?
- What sort of sacred space can best remind us to look to the One within?
- How can the relationship with the environment help link us to the One without?
- How will the design reflect interdependence with community?
- How can the entire project serve as a vehicle for the Journey?

Myths do not have to be ancient fairy tales to be true, and though we may not think of ourselves as mythmakers, no one will deny that every house is the representation of the consciousness of its owner and designer. Let's look at an example of how this can work for us. If my truth is that I am striving to live in harmony with the environment, then my built myth might take the form of a solar house with roofwater collection, natural and non-toxic materials, and xeriscapic gardens. Windows and doors might be placed to attune me to the rhythms of sunrise and sunset. Bedrooms might be intimate and sensuous spaces well-suited for dreams and intimacy. If I am a musician, I might place the music room or the piano at the heart of the house. And if preparing food is a special, almost sacramental activity for me, I might emphasize the sacred quality of the ancient hearth with a beautiful treatment of the area surrounding the kitchen stove.

To call this "built myth" is not mere semantics. It's really saying that we are going to create a mythic realm which is so powerfully alive with spirit, shapes, patterns of movement and energies that one will actually experience the journey for which the house is a vehicle. The very moment someone walks in the front door, we want them to feel that they are entering a transcendent or magical realm, leaving mundane existence behind. We are, in fact, creating a transformation of consciousness. Designing a house as built myth is thus an easy and wonderful way of focusing intention, to which we must now add form and energy.

ARCHETYPE, SYMBOL, AND ENERGY

Chapter Three

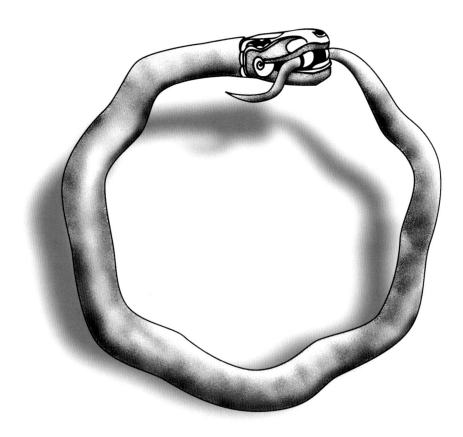

The serpent, symbol of nature in its most primal form, swallows its own tail. Death is followed by rebirth in an endless continuum which forms the sacred circle of wholeness.

Though we may not be able to articulate it, we all know the difference between a building which is vibrant and full of energy and one which feels lifeless. Whereas some buildings are cold, hollow and even frightening, a structure with energy can awaken us, lift our spirits, and move us to laughter or tears.

By what alchemy does a pile of stones become, in effect, a living structure? It might be supposed that there are visible or measurable features which create energy. We could look for design elements such as the play of light, the sense of proportion, or the use of color and texture. We could examine how the house is sited, how views are framed, or how space is enclosed. We might perform a *feng shui* analysis, or a comparison with classic forms of sacred geometry. Yet beyond all these quantifiable elements, there remains an intangible essence which can not be measured, taught, nor produced by formula. No amount of scientific measurement will detect the energy we feel, nor determine how it might have come to be there.

So now we add to our journey a mystery: a search for an entity which, as it were, breathes life into stones! It is time to visit the archetypes.

The Archetypes

"Archetype," according to the dictionary, refers to an original pattern or model, a first form, or a prototype. The ancient idea is that behind every observable form or phenomenon is an idealized form or template, living on another plane of existence — thus, although there may be thousands or millions of nurturing mothers on earth at any given moment, there exists just one archetype of the Great Mother which provides the potential for all earthly mothers. Both the name and the concept of archetype go back to ancient Greek times, and many thinkers from Plato to Augustine had explored this territory by the time Carl Gustav Jung took up the thread in the early part of this century.

Jung's theory of the collective unconscious actually grew from a dream of a house. (This in itself has enormous significance for us house lovers, and we'll return to this dream in Chapter Six). In this house the upper story represented the conscious mind, while the lower three depicted successively deeper levels of the unconscious. What he noticed in particular was that the lowest two contained detail indicating a *collective* or *universal* quality.

This was the genesis of Jung's big breakthrough, which he developed and refined over more than half a century. Previously, Freud had identified the *personal* unconscious, that repository of repressed biographical material and memories originating in post-natal experience. But the concept of the *collective* unconscious was something entirely new, and carried with it profound implications. For one, the theory says that the collective unconscious is a *substrate* which underlies and precedes consciousness — implying that it has a life of its own, older than and quite beyond the reach of our conscious minds. Second, it is a limitless, timeless and primordial psychic realm which we *all* inherit along with our genes. Third, we all share the *same* unconscious. Last, the collective unconscious is enormously powerful and dynamic, and is capable of projecting itself into the conscious world and acting upon us, most obviously in the case of the instincts.

Jung's writings abound with anecdotes suggesting how powerful the contents of the unconscious are. What a sobering notion that an immense and potent entity dwells within and can powerfully influence us, whereas ordinarily we can't even see it, let alone control it! For primitive man, whose consciousness was relatively newborn and weak, it appeared to be a matter of sheer survival to hold such forces at bay — as we have seen, this was how myth and ritual began. However for us, possessing as we do a more stabilized ego, to integrate the unconscious with consciousness in a more or less orderly way is what Jung called the process of individuation, or the path to the Self. In other words, whereas we think of ourselves as being exclusively the conscious personality, the truth is that we are also our unconscious, with which the conscious mind must be integrated or harmonized for us to be whole.

What, according to Jung, are the contents of the collective unconscious? The archetypes, of course! Initially Jung recognized them as "forms of instinct," but in time he came to understand them as fundamental, universal and unimaginably potent psychic patterns, forces, or (in words which sound much like quantum physics) "tendencies to exist." The archetypes include the fundamental laws of Nature, but they also rule our own human nature. So in contacting the archetypes there is enormous potential to bring these two natures into harmony, granting the transformation, healing and creativity which are the goals of Archetype Design.

Jung's enormous contribution has deservedly dominated the domain of archetypal psychology to this day — so much so, that any discussion of the archetypes inevitably takes as a baseline the groundbreaking work which he provided. However, it is timely to point out that the Jungians by no means have the last word. Thus in Chapter Five we will move on to the view of transpersonal psychology which expands considerably beyond the predominantly Jungian approach we are examining in this chapter.

The Personified Archetypes

For the purposes of our work we can divide the archetypes into two categories. The first are those which can be personified or visualized as some sort of larger-than-life beings. Examples are the Great Mother, the Shadow, the Anima and the Animus, the Trickster, the Wise Old Man or Woman, and the Hero. Frequently they take different names and identities in the great myths, and that generally is how we come to know them. But it is extremely important to understand that *any image or name we ascribe to an archetype is merely a construct of our own*: such names or forms vary greatly by individual and by culture and may tell as much about the perceiver as the perceived. No one has ever seen an archetype — the closest we come is our imaginings and our renderings in storytelling and art. The same Trickster is Coyote to Native Americans and the Jester of the Tarot. The identical Virgin was revered as Isis by the Egyptians and as Mary by the Christians. The Hero has appeared as Christ and Buddha, as Percival, Theseus, and Luke Skywalker. So, while we can't directly see the archetype, by comparing the representations in the different myths we can begin to get a feel for the underlying essence which consistently animates the various images.

Strictly speaking, the personified archetypes have no particular relationship to architecture — it is the symbolized archetypes of transformation, which we will examine next, which relate much more directly to our design work. However, when we enter the archetypal realm we are opening ourselves equally to all the archetypes, and so we should be prepared to encounter any one of them. Moreover, the personified archetypes can assist us enormously in the area of personal transformation, which is, in fact, the primary goal of the Journey.

Wherever there is a manifest human trait or tendency, there lies behind it an archetype – in plain talk, one might say that we are simply wired up to behave in certain ways. This is why certain works of art can speak to us across centuries of cultural differences, or why our emotional nature is fundamentally the same worldwide. However, the archetypes are immeasurably more powerful than we are, and the notions of instincts, or of genetic predisposition, or even of being "wired up" – however correct they may be – don't even begin to convey the enormous potential of coming into accord with the archetypes and using their energy for our own transformation and creativity.

Thus, to recognize the archetypes and sense them at work within us is the beginning of a new archetypal awareness. For example, when we feel a heroic impulse swelling up within us and carrying us beyond the usual human scale towards something greater than ourselves, we can take it that the Hero is at work. The next step in the process might be to intentionally call up that archetype at another moment when we need such heroic energy and wish to activate the same potential in ourselves. In time, we may discover that the archetypal Hero's journey as described in world mythology in fact provides a template for our own Journey towards wholeness. The thresholds and transformations along our life path may be experienced as the perennial signposts of the one metamyth, and to the degree that we give ourselves to the Journey, the energy and transformation we experience can approach heroic proportions.

Similarly, when an old woman appears to us in a dream, we can instantly recognize Wise Woman and pay close attention to the message she bears. We can benefit enormously from becoming familiar with such energies, rather than remaining puzzled, frightened, or merely indifferent. Taken deeply, this work with the archetypes can become very healing. For example, a man's relationship with women may be utterly transformed as he begins to interact with the Anima (his own feminine side) and hears his own feminine nature speaking to him in the guise of individual women.

However, it is important to understand that opening the door to the archetypes promises a wild ride. For example, the unconscious realm is spectacularly unconcerned with the conventions of good and bad which fragment consensus reality. Whereas we may have repressed the deathly, dark, and frightening elements of experience, these have free rein in the unconscious, which is undivided in this regard. Here, wrathful deities exist in equal number to the benevolent ones

— and it should come as no surprise if these repressed denizens of the psyche are clamoring for attention. For this reason it is not uncommon that at the beginning of the journey the scenery is dominated by the wild and dark elements of the psyche.

Working with the archetypes requires courage, stability of mind, and a strong sense of "center." It is a tumultuous cast of characters we are inviting in: the archetypes have their own logic and generally do not oblige us by behaving according to our rules and timetable. It is essential to be prepared to receive whatever experience arises and to discern the forces at work. Thus when we feel utterly overwhelmed by chaos, when everything seems to be falling apart, or when the ego is being shattered, the *ability to detect an element of grace or intelligence at work* may be what enables us to persevere. In such moments it can be absolutely transformative to feel that Kali is having her way with us, or that the Trickster is bestowing his crazy wisdom, or that the pagaent of death-and-rebirth is once again playing out its timeless theme on the stage of our own psyches. At times when we are utterly out of control, awash in terror or confusion, we very quickly appreciate how myth originally arose as a way of explaining the unexplainable.

Paradoxically, the unconscious which we regard with such fear is fundamentally healing:

> **"Normally the unconscious collaborates with the conscious without friction or disturbance, so that one is not even aware of its existence. But when an individual or a social group deviates too far from their instinctual foundations, they then experience the full impact of unconscious forces. The collaboration of the unconscious is intelligent and purposive, and even when it acts in opposition to consciousness its expression is still compensatory in an intelligent way, as if it were trying to restore the lost balance."**
> — C.G. Jung, *The Archetypes and the Collective Unconscious* p.282

We can liken the archetypes to the ocean waves whose destructive potential we rightly fear: though we can't control the waves, we can ride them, we can harness their power, and we can also listen for our Self in the music of the breakers and rhythm of the tides. Above all, we must not be so foolish as to ignore them. Without them, the sea of existence would be a bleak and featureless place.

There remains another aspect of the archetypes to consider — a disturbing one, pertaining to conditions when entire populations are in the grip of seeming madness. Jung described the Nazi phenomenon thus in 1936:

> *"There are as many archetypes as there are typical situations in life...the archetype corresponding to a situation becomes activated, and as a result those explosive and dangerous forces hidden in the archetype come into action, frequently with unpredictable consequences...if thirty years ago anyone had dared to predict that our psychological development was tending towards a revival of the medieval perseceutions of the Jews, that Europe would again tremble before the Roman fasces and the tramp of legions, that people would once again give the Roman salute, as two thousand years ago, and that instead of the Christian cross an archaic swastika would lure onwards millions of warriors ready for death - why, that man would have been hooted as a mystical fool."*
>
> — C.G. Jung, *The Archetypes and the Collective Unconscious*, p.47-48

In his later years Jung made similar observations about the Cold War, and we could safely extend the same thinking to our present predicament: what sort of madness can possess entire cultures to actually consume and pollute both themselves and the planet? Is there a clue here which points the way to healing?

The answer is: Yes there is a clue, because when we split off part of our inner nature there will be inevitable consequences in our relationship to the corresponding nature outside ourselves. For example, if we banish our primitive, feeling and nurturing faculties, it is predictable that we will relate to the natural world and to other humans in unfeeling and destructive ways. Moreover, the archetypal energies which are thus repressed may indeed develop explosive potential, sometimes manifesting as their opposite, or Shadow, which tugs at our awareness as a prod to restore the lost balance. Far too often we respond by exerting additional energy to keep the Shadow at bay, even as our sense of fear increases and we respond irrationally to emergent conditions in the world. So it is that, feeling insecure and afraid, we react instantly and aggressively to real or imagined threats, only compounding the situation and giving us seeming justification for our fears. This of course, is the national experience over the past several decades.

In our own time, much of world society is divided along lines of race and fundamentalist dogma; we are globally locked in struggles for economic domination, and personal hungers override any concern for others and for the environment. This looks remarkably like a group which is deeply frightened and is desperately seeking refuge behind mental or material bastions. Efforts at reconciliation and co-operation fail or are short-lived because we are yet to do the work of reclaiming the feeling and nurturing qualities which can connect us to the environment and to each other. So to journey inside — to face the Shadow and reclaim that which we have split off — is actually the prerequisite without which both personal and collective healing is impossible. The seeds of aggression, greed, and ignorance must be confronted inside rather than played out on the stage of the world.

Let's review just a bit. Since the earliest times man has struggled to consolidate and sharpen the conscious mind, with the result that we have erected a considerable array of defenses against intrusion by the archetypes which dwell in the unconscious. Only in the case of mental illness do they generally burst upon our conscious life. But though we think our defenses offer safety, it is a false security at best, and one which leaves us impoverished. The security is false because our denial leaves us susceptible to the kind of mass psychosis which possesses us even now. And we are left impoverished because, lacking a bridge to the unconscious, we deprive ourselves of the very primordial legacy which we need to heal ourselves and become whole.

Creating such a bridge to the unconscious is the all-important first step in our work of healing. At the same time it is the essential experiential component of Archetype Design because, as we are beginning to see, the unconscious is the primary source of energy and creativity.

Is it too optimistic to think that human beings are finally ready to do the work of uniting the unconscious and the conscious? Certainly not: after millennia of evolution our minds are more than stable enough to hold onto our hats as we cautiously open the door to the archetypes. We are motivated by a fast-growing awareness that our very survival is at stake. Most importantly, we are rediscovering the tools — the "technologies of the sacred" — to shape our consciousness so that, very gradually, we can relax the frightened ego and take our seat at the Center. Here we can rest, allowing the unconscious and the conscious elements to integrate.

The Archetypes of Transformation

The second category of archetypes are those of *transformation*, which provide the maps to the terrain we traverse as we integrate the conscious and unconscious elements.

Whereas the personified archetypes are like huge unseen actors, the archetypes of transformation are the templates or ordering principles of nature. They have been traditionally rendered as *symbols* and typically take elemental or cosmic forms. Each chapter of this book begins with one such symbol. Examples include the archetype of the unconscious (symbolized by water) or the archetype of life (the tree). The archetype of wholeness, which is similar to the archetype of the Self, is symbolized by the circle. The Sacred Journey is symbolized by the spiral, while the related vortex and labyrinth often symbolize lowerworld journeys. The archetype of the center of the world is the world mountain, sometimes represented as a pyramid or as world tree or pillar. The number three and the triangle are archetypes of the divine. The number four is an archetype of the forces of nature, frequently rendered as the quadrated circle, a dynamic representation of the one-and-the-many. Seven is the number of the chakras, frequently reflected in seven-tiered pagodas or stepped pyramids. The *yoni* is the archetype of birth and transformation and is symbolized by the door or passageway. Fire is the alchemical agent of transformation and holds a key place in both primitive and contemporary dwellings. Suddenly, we find ourselves in a world of symbolized "first forms," many of which are the very stuff of architecture.

This, of course, is the motherlode of Archetype Design from which this work took its original inspiration. The archetypes of transformation encode the most basic patterns and laws of the universe: math, architecture, physics, music and geometry are all here in seed form — and they are as close to us as our own breath. Many of them are complete architectural forms, unambiguously showing how we can infuse our buildings with the transformative and healing properties of the very ordering principles of nature. Worldwide, and as far back as Neolithic times, these principles have informed sacred architecture as spirals, pyramids, quadrated circles, and sacred proportions — and they are precisely the energies we seek to tap.

It is important to underscore how central such symbols are in the Jungian view. The Self is precisely the totality of the conscious and the unconscious, and *symbols are the primary vehicle for uniting the two*:

> *"How the harmonizing of conscious and unconscious data is to be undertaken cannot be indicated in the form of a recipe. It is an irrational life-process which expresses itself in definite symbols...knowledge of the symbols is indispensable, for it is in them that the union of conscious and unconscious contents is consummated."*
>
> — C.G. Jung, *The Archetypes and The Collective Unconscious*, p. 289

The contemplation of the symbols of transformation, and particularly spontaneous drawing or visualizing of them, is a primary method of psychic integration. Thus it should come as no surprise that sacred architecture is filled with the forms of pyramids, quadrated circles, crosses, spirals, rosettes, lotuses, sunbursts, domes, arches and pillars. Here the Sacred Journey and architecture are one and the same, and although our homes represent a different myth and in most cases will not look like temples or cathedrals, they may nevertheless encode the energies of sacred symbols in subtle ways. Without a doubt, coming to the drawing board steeped in the experience of archetypal symbols is going to generate a far different result from being steeped only in images from the homes of movie stars.

How we actually gain access to the archetypes is the subject of later chapters. For now, let us return to our mystery of living stones: if, somehow, the enormous potency of the archetypes could be rendered in stone, then this might be as close as we can get to having those stones actually come to life. The contents of the unconscious live in all of us, so it is certain that if an architect can succeed in rendering that essence in a building, then any one of us has the ability to recognize and feel that living energy and its dynamic, transformative properties.

Energy

While it is not possible to see an archetype or render it literally, it is possible to feel and communicate the energy or emotion associated with it. Recall Perry's description of the origin of myth and the dual aspect of image and emotion in Chapter Two. Jung addresses the same dynamic as follows:

> *"The archetypes...are pieces of life itself – images that are integrally connected to the living individual by the bridge of the emotions. They are, at the same time, both images and emotions. One can speak of an archetype only when these two aspects are simultaneous. When there is merely the image, then there is simply a word-picture of little consequence. But by being charged with emotion, the image gains numinosity (or psychic energy); it becomes dynamic, and consequences of some kind must flow from it...They gain life and meaning only when you try to take into account their numinosity – ie ., their relationship to the living individual."*
>
> — C.G. Jung, *Man & His Symbols*, p.96ff

In other words, the energy in an image is communicated through the emotional value it carries for an individual. This can occur at many levels. Most superficially, the emotional experience of an object will vary from individual to individual according to cultural conditioning: the symbol of the cross means one thing to a Congolese tribeswoman and something entirely different to a European. Experience may also be dictated by the consciousness of the viewer: a pilgrim may see the divine in a statue of the Virgin, while a rapist may see only sexual characteristics. However, though individual consciousness or conditioning may determine how a symbol is received, *only archetypal symbols are capable of broadcasting at the deepest non-verbal, preconscious level and with the greatest amount of energy.*

In short, the deeper we are able to go with our own awareness, the deeper will be our experience of the archetypes and the potential for personal transformation. Then, too, will we have the greatest opportunity to bring this energy back into the forms of architecture.

Jung termed the energy of which we have been speaking *numinosity*. Anthropologists call it *mana*, connoting a supernatural or divine power which is concentrated in an object or a being. The Taoists call it *chi*, while the yogis in India term it *shakti* or *prana*. In other words, the same basic energy is differently understood and labeled in the different cultures, while the various myths and wisdom traditions provide diverse templates for experiencing it. They are all valid, and each adds welcome depth to our own pale word "energy."

Awareness of the sacred or transformational quality of energy has been somewhat neglected in the West, having been long ago relegated to the domain of alchemy and the occult arts. We prefer the materialist view of energy, calling it mass times velocity squared and leaving it at that. But in Asia and older cultures, energy has retained its sacred connotations and is very much part of everyday reality. In India, it is taken for granted that we can feel the energy of a building, a place, or a person, and be very much affected by it. In primitive cultures, where the people are acutely attuned to the natural surroundings, energy sensors are most finely honed: in the jungle, for instance, the ability to sense predator or prey can mean the difference between life and death. All of us are genetically endowed with the same ability: far from being hocus-pocus, energy awareness is largely a function of practice. For example, in this country dowsers have never stopped using their sensitivity to reliably find underground water. And as any practitioner of *reiki* or acupuncture can affirm, the ability to sense energy flow in the body is simply a matter of paying attention.

Energy can sometimes be felt as a current, similar to electricity. There may be a vibrating quality, or sensations of warmth or of pleasure. Some individuals are capable of seeing subtle energy fields or auras. Closing the eyes, we may experience similar light qualities. Listening attentively, we may detect sound. The depth and speed of the breath may change in the presence of different energy fields, as may body temperature. Affective qualities can range from soothing to extremely excitatory.

Part of our work is therefore to develop the subtle intuitive or *feeling* center. At one level, this dovetails with the familiar effort to be "in touch with our feelings" which has absorbed our culture for two or three decades. Simply changing language from thinking words to feeling words is actually a potent step in this regard. But as we take the process deeper, we actually initiate more radical shifts: from thought to feeling, from logic to intuition, from word to image, from left brain to right brain. In later chapters we will explore techniques for creating this shift with relative ease.

If symbols (image) operate on us through emotion, then energy awareness and emotional rather than mental focus are principal tools for becoming fluent in the language of image and metaphor. The next step is one of intention: we must really be willing to plumb our creative depths in order to strike the motherlode and experience archetypal energies and symbols in all their raw potency. Jung stated the point concisely, describing symbols as

> *". . .very bold attempts to see and put together apparently irreconcilable opposites and bridge over apparently hopeless splits. Even the mere attempt in this direction usually has a healing effect, but only when it is done spontaneously. Nothing can be expected from an artificial repetition or a deliberate imitation of such images."*
> - C.G. Jung, *The Archetypes and the Collective Unconscious*, p. 390

It cannot be overemphasized that the *potency of archetypal patterns and symbols comes only from direct inner experience*. To simply understand the symbols intellectually is to confer meaning without energy; to merely copy the symbols and forms of yore is to deal in clichés. Thus Archetype Design can never be a matter of designing by formula. This requires some discipline in a consumer culture where the media and the marketplace offer so many instant, off-the-shelf options. For example, now that we know that the archetype of wholeness is symbolized by a circle, it is tempting to suppose that we can slap together a circular structure like Black Elk's, call it sacred geometry, and all will be well. But the result would simply be a circle without energy, a hollow cliché, because the design will have come from wishful thinking rather than from spontaneous inner process. To get authentic substance rather than mere style requires deep work.

We have identified a primal source of energy (the unconscious and the archetypes), we have cultivated our ability to feel energy, and we have formed the intention to let architectural forms grow "from the forgotten depths." We are getting closer to the mystery of investing stones with energy.

Art & Make-Believe

To the extent that we succeed in shifting from ordinary linear thinking to right-brain, intuitive, feeling consciousness, architecture becomes more art than science. Accordingly, it becomes useful to refer to questions about the mystery of art which long have absorbed our best thinkers.

Joseph Campbell considers the phenomenon of aesthetic arrest – the aha! experience – by drawing from works by St. Thomas Aquinas and James Joyce. Using the analogy of music, Aquinas described how the various parts of an art object relate to each other and to the whole through *rhythm*. When the artist gets it all just right, the result is *harmony*, and this in turn creates an energy he calls *radiance*. And radiance is that quality of Suchness or perfection which touches the Suchness at the core of our being, causing us to stand stockstill and become absorbed in the moment. (Joseph Campbell, *The Mythic Dimension*, p.193-4)

Campbell asks why we are able to experience harmony and radiance this way, and answers: because the harmony is the harmony of *our* nature, which is the same as the nature outside. And the radiance is likewise the radiance of *our* nature, which is the same as the nature outside. The analogy of sympathetic strings is a good one: we are simply wired up to respond to the vibration of Suchness whenever we come into its presence in a work of art, in nature, or in another human being, because that same Suchness is already present in us as archetype.

It is interesting that we so often resort to musical terms in describing visual art. The reason is that art is ultimately not a mechanical process which we can package and produce. Art is a bridge to other dimensions – a mystery – and, in the way of mysteries, we have to talk around it with image and metaphor while the actual magic of art remains hidden. Perhaps this is why Campbell calls artists the mythmakers of our day: as life becomes increasingly secular, art is virtually the last surviving stronghold of magic and mystery. And this, of course, is the proper function of architecture as well.

In India it is understood that the gift of the artist is his ability to journey to *Satloka*, the transcendent realm of Truth, and to bring back to this world the pure vision which his skill can then render in stone. He journeys to Satloka because he feels the call, and he refines the ability to travel there through meditation and spiritual practice. But how he can bring back the archetype and render it in stone, nobody knows. Some things are simply better left as mystery.

So it is with myth as well. Rituals (which are nothing less than re-enacted myths) work because of the participants' willingness to suspend the grip of the rational mind and enter a mythic realm where time and space fall away and we are once again in Satloka. In effect this is another state of consciousness, a non-ordinary or altered state such as shamans and medicine women have aspired to for countless centuries. Such states are hardly far removed from any of our experience: all of us as children understood completely the magical power of fantasy and make-believe (frequently enacted, one might add, in doll houses and playhouses of all kinds). Once again we are left holding a mystery, for although we return to ordinary consciousness transfigured, we simply cannot say with any precision how we did so. Although researchers can measure changes in pulse and brain waves, the actual mechanics of change of consciousness remain beyond our analytical abilities. The best we can do is simply learn to take the journey and to return, integrating whatever treasure we are able to bring back.

Investing Energy

We would be leaving a gaping hole in our discussion if we failed to consider the everyday process of investing a building with energy. For example, the housewarming is simply a ritual, albeit a secularized one, of breathing life into a house. Traditionally there have been other ceremonies or rites of passage for a house, including the groundbreaking to dedicate the site and the topping-off ceremony to mark the raising of the roof. Conversely, we perform clearing rituals and exorcisms to rid homes of stagnant, malevolent energy or of unwanted spirits.

All such rituals presuppose that we have the ability to affect the energy or vibration of our built environment. The effectiveness of focused energy is well demonstrated by the transformation in an old house which we might rent or purchase: frequently the building starts out with musty, spooky or stagnated energy, but within months the house develops a lively, luminous and animated feeling. Somehow the thoughts, emotions, and energy which emanate from us become stored in our surroundings. Once again we are obliged to speak of mystery — yet why should we ever regard as strange the proposition that energy coming from our bodies, which after all are comprised of earth elements, can be registered in the earth elements around us?

Whether we occupy an older structure bearing someone else's vibrations, or a new house of our own conscious design, we will powerfully affect the space as we live in it. If we truly use the kitchen as a place of healing, that energy will build. If our intention is to become purified in the bathroom, that quality will actually increase. And if in fact we use the house as a vehicle for spirit, it is inevitable that healing and uplifting energy will build over time.

TRANSFORMATION AND THE CREATIVE PROCESS

Chapter Four

Also called the Tai Chi, the Yin-Yang represents the interplay of the cosmic opposites within the sacred circle. The dark is Yang, the masculine or the Creative. The light is Yin, the feminine or the Receptive. Though opposites, the seed of each aspect is to be found emerging from directly within the other. By merging with this archetype through profound receptivity, one becomes transparent to the Creative.

C reativity, judging from the huge volume of books and seminars on the topic, is a most highly-prized gift in our culture. But a closer look reveals the degree to which the literature on creativity reflects our materialist bias. Most of the available material is directed towards commercial success, such as how to produce inventive and profitable objects and ideas. Famous artists are celebrated as cultural icons alongside movie stars, but they are frequently lauded as much for their success in the marketplace as for what their art is actually saying. Creativity itself is marketed as a commodity. This is the state of creativity in the absence of the sacred.

It has not always been thus. The *I Ching*, for example, begins with two hexagrams *The Creative* and *The Receptive*. Graphically they are represented by the Yin / Yang, which is an archetypal symbol of transformation *par excellence*. The Creative (yang) is the principle of energy expanding and taking form, while the Receptive (yin) is the energy of the feminine, of potential, of the unconscious. The tiny dots in the symbol are the seeds of each quality arising within the other in a perfectly balanced dynamic or interplay of opposites. So the Creative is one side of the universe, half of the divine pair which manifests as the dance of life. And from where does the Creative emerge? From deep inside the Receptive herself.

There could hardly be a view of creativity in more marked contrast to the prevailing mainstream bias. Whereas the conventional view is that creativity is a skill to be acquired from without, this view states unequivocally that creativity is a primordial principle of the universe, to be found deep within ourselves.

In a universe composed of Yin and Yang, to gain access to the Creative principle we have to penetrate the core of the Receptive. Such an endeavor is quite different from learning to be receptive in the academic sense — rather, it is a matter of systematically going beyond the ego into new dimensions of the Self. In effect, the ego and our entire sense of self must momentarily dissolve, allowing our consciousness to go through the "eye of the needle" and actually dive directly into the archetype of transformation. This is far from an intellectual exercise: to pass through the eye of the needle we have to strip down, leaving behind memory, intellect, fear and desire. Even the wish to be more creative is an obstacle at this point.

Of course, having stripped ourselves naked and having plunged into the abyss, something is bound to happen to us, and that "something" is going to be a powerful personal transformation. In mythological terms, it is the Hero's journey repeated all over again: we may return from our quest with the holy grail of creativity, but not before we have surmounted herculean challenges of the sort which will forever change us.

At just this point some readers may raise the objection: but what about creative geniuses like Mozart, or Einstein, or Picasso? If they produced such incredible work without taking journeys of transformation, why can't we?

To answer this we must refer back to our original intention, which is one of both creativity and transformation. If one simply intends to bring dazzling inventiveness to one's work, then quite possibly this can be accomplished by dint of effort, talent, and originality. Creativity in this sense is exactly the commodity of which we have spoken, and may indeed be ten percent inspiration and ninety percent perspiration as Thomas Edison reported. But the creativity we are exploring in Archetype Design is of another order entirely, because our intention is primarily one of healing, or of returning to wholeness. Here *transformation* is the ultimate goal, and creativity is both a catalyst and a by-product. The Creative, in short, is (in tandem with the Receptive) the primal energy which drives transformation, and transformation itself is synonymous with *creating new forms out of the old.*

In the rush to be successful and productive, the need to pair transformation with creativity is generally overlooked. But when creativity is developed in the absence of personal transformation, the result is often what we call the mad scientist or the crazy artist. This can be easily understood in terms of the archetypes, which penetrate our defenses in moments of mental instability such as sleep, daydream, or emotional distress. The result can be displays of highly charged and vivid imagery which bespeak the archetypal realm. When portrayed on canvas or on celluloid, the resulting art can be provocative and extremely moving. And when superb technique is added to the formula, then we toast the work as "good" art, never asking ourselves whether the art is as healing as it is accomplished.

Certainly there *is* something inherently healing about all artistic expression. Art is a most powerful tool for connecting us with inner forces and giving expression to image-and-emotion. Art can be healing for both the artist and the viewer, so not for a moment should art of any kind be denigrated. However, when the intention is a limited one of art-for-art's-sake rather than of healing transformation, there will inevitably be a corresponding limit to the healing which is available.

So if our intention is to create architecture which heals — and to be healed even as we create — then clearly we are exploring a special sort of creativity which goes beyond inventiveness. We do well, then, to speak in terms of the Creative, because this is creativity at the level of fundamental life principle, or archetype. Now what we are wanting from the Creative seems to be two things. First, we seek to heal ourselves and become whole. Second — or simultaneously, rather — we seek to portray both the journey and the goal in the design of our homes, and to do so in a beautiful and new way which expresses our unique selves.

When we invoke the Creative we also get the Receptive, and together they generate wholeness, whether it is the wholeness of the nature within us or of nature outside. So it seems likely that the dynamic of Yin/Yang is indeed capable of generating both the healing we seek and the creative image-and-emotion which will inform our design. Of course we'll have to add a little technique in order to get it all right, first on paper and then in stone — but that is in the realm of mastery, which we will reserve for Part Two.

Let's return to our archetype of transformation and its symbol, the Yin/Yang. We have already commented that the Creative (which creates form) emerges from the Receptive (which is the formless). New forms are continuously emerging from the formless, all of which goes on quite nicely without us. But then we come along to enter this dance, and two things simultaneously occur. We experience a transformation in ourselves, and somehow we also become agents of the Creative.

The dynamic of this transformation is an important one. To begin with, a shift in consciousness accompanies our descent into the archetype; for example, the everyday linear left-brain consciousness must be temporarily abandoned, enabling the shift into the intuitive and imaging right-brain. As we descend deeper, we momentarily lose our ordinary sense of body-and-mind. At this point the simple fact is that we don't know exactly who or where we will be when the journey is over. It's very much like the Uncertainty Principle in quantum physics:

when particles are shot from point A to point B, we can't really see the particles while they are in transit. We can observe either their mass or their velocity, but we can't measure both at once, which is the same as saying that the particles seem to be there but we can't quite confirm it. Moreover, it can't be predicted for sure just where the particles will strike or what they will look like when they get there. Our status as we explore the archetypes is just the same.

So why would we risk a leap into an experience in which we don't know where we are or who we will become? First of all, we do it because it's the only way to reach this particular goal. Second, we stick with the process, however uncomfortable it may be at times, because we are reassured by the presence of an inherently safe and healing energy which guides and protects us. Mythologically, it is the hand of the divine messenger or goddess. Experience confirms that there is an innate intelligence at work which takes us unerringly where we need to go. After all, this is a fundamental ordering principle of the universe to which we are submitting — so it had better be good for something even as we seek it out! With a little experience, and perhaps a bit of guidance, we learn to trust the process. Finally, this is an adventure which is incredibly fun and yet delivers a big payoff: *for each time the form of our solid ego-mind dissolves, we become transparent to The Creative.* The result is spontaneous and effortless creativity which we bring back with us when our consciousness consolidates once again. Nothing at all is acquired or learned, yet we return steeped in primordial creative energy.

The process is utterly simple and self-reinforcing. The more we open to transformation the more we are healed, the more we become transparent to The Creative, and the more we are inclined to repeat the journey. In Chapter Five we will explore the various techniques for dissolving our solid identity and inviting the creative experience.

There are other aspects of transformation which are worth noting, such as Picasso's famous remark that every creative act begins with an act of destruction. In the context of our work this means that our own form (of solidified consciousness) has to dissolve — to actually be destroyed — in order for a creative transformation to take place. When that dissolution takes place, energy is released much as when molecules and atoms are split, and we may experience remarkable rapture, excitement, or serenity. These energies themselves are extremely healing and tend to trigger other events or states of mind such as unity or cosmic consciousness, boundless compassion, or creative insight.

Seen from another point of view, the process of transformation is one of ego death-and-rebirth. We know by now that death-and-rebirth is a central archetypal theme, globally re-enacted since earliest times in myth and ritual. So when we participate in this mystery through inner journey and intentional ego death, we are precisely reliving the primal act of creation. We are in direct contact with immense energies. When we touch the Creative on this basis, to ever again pursue creativity in the conventional sense becomes completely superfluous.

Finally: as the energy of the Creative flows through us, it is inevitably shaped or conditioned by our myriad human qualities, so we can be confident that the work we produce will be just as unique as we are. There is absolutely no need to struggle to be either unique or creative. All we have to do is continue the journey of transformation, and to do so authentically.

Mystery vs. Mastery

A perpetual dilemma which we face on the Journey — whether we view it as the journey of transformation or the journey of creative expression — is how to keep creativity from being stifled either by formalism or by the mind's need to be productive. There is an urgency, particularly in our culture, to get the job done and have something to show for our efforts. Not only do we rush to produce concrete results, but in so doing we tend to settle for off-the-shelf formulas for both creative work and spiritual practice. Yet it should be clear by now that both transformation and creativity are creatures of process, not to be nicely packaged according to expectations nor delivered on time.

Just as we are all familiar with the difference between living spirit and orthodoxy, so in other areas we seesaw between an irrational and penetrating intuition and an intellect which is precise but arid. We speak, for example, of art versus science. In design work, the creative dilemma typically presents itself as the struggle between sheer creative expression and methodical problem-solving, or between fresh inspiration and tried-and-tested formulae. In this book we comment frequently on the theme of mystery and mastery, and acknowledge that sooner or later every inspired insight must pass through the filter of reality testing so that we can be sure our ideas will work. Oftentimes this entails a constant back-and-forth game of creative work balanced by reality checks. But the all-important point is not to stifle creativity with practical considerations. Hence we must take care to reserve mastery for the right time, embracing the Taoist ideal of remaining still until the moment of action.

Architecture is laden with systems and formulas for design, which in our arena include sustainability techniques, *feng shui, stapatya veda*, and sacred geometry. Clearly it is worthwhile to study any of these systems. General building knowledge prepares us to envision designs which can actually be built, while familiarity with sustainable building methods will ground us in an orientation to the earth and the elements. Exploring *feng shui* will enhance our awareness of energy flow, while sacred geometry will attune our minds to fundamental ordering principles of the cosmos. All such training can be invaluable — but in the creative process, mastery can be an impediment if we fail to suspend it in favor of mystery.

As Jung spoke of the need to allow archetypal symbols to emerge from the forgotten depths of the psyche, so in Archetype Design we emphasize the value of letting both creative vision and our own emerging sense of self arise spontaneously from the inner journey. This accords with the traditional model of the creative process, which identifies three phases: initially a set of conditions or problems is encountered and explored; there follows a fallow or unfocused period during which the problem is largely put on the back burner; finally, the "eureka!" moment spontaneously arises when the creative solution presents itself, seemingly out of nowhere. There is general agreement about this description, to which are added personal touches: Mozart's accounts of pleasant rides in the countryside prior to composing, Einstein perceiving the special theory of relativity kinesthetically through sensations in his arm, and Newton's famous apple bonking him on the head. The essential point, however, seems to be that the creative impulse emerges spontaneously out of the void.

In the past several decades psychologists have mounted countless studies intended to unlock the secrets of the creative process. For example, creativity has been correlated with intelligence up to the threshold of IQ 120, but it has not been shown that intelligence is a reliable predictor of creativity. Tests to measure creativity have been developed, with varying validity and success. Similarly, while attempts have been made to correlate creativity with personality, motivation, or childhood experiences, the creative process remains an elusive quarry.

The pitfall in such research is that it may be tinged by our cultural preoccupation with success and achievement. To the extent that they focus on celebrities considered to be at a lofty level of genius, these studies may reinforce the thought that such creativity is beyond the reach of us ordinary folks. This can be damaging. Moreover, the idea of creativity as some sort of externalized attribute may also be strengthened. So the proper attitude is to ask the simple question: what insights are available which can help maximize my creativity just as I am? If indeed the sources of creative process lie inside the psyche, how can I succeed in releasing them?

Gardners's *Creating Minds* offers us this general picture of famously "creative" people: They come from supportive but rather normal families, they take a relatively early interest in their life's work, and they devote perhaps ten years or more to mastering this domain. At the critical moment the creative exemplar encounters a central problem and responds with a sweeping, radical, and unforeseeable solution, often redefining the very domain in which he or she is working. During the creative period he or she enjoys cognitive support from at least one associate as well as emotional support from a spouse or near one. Finally, this creative person becomes totally absorbed in the work, even to the complete detriment of relationships or of what we usually consider a balanced life.

While there are some lessons to learn from the lives of creative people, we don't come away with a sure-fire template for becoming creative ourselves. Imitating Einstein is not going to make one into a great physicist — fully being oneself might be much more helpful! Then, too, we might ask ourselves if we are willing to trade away our relationships for our work — when, in fact, relationships may well *be* our work. Yet we can also see ways in which the design process easily conforms to Gardner's description: house design is famously all-consuming, and since homes are usually designed for two there is certainly the opportunity for cognitive and emotional support.

Two other observations in the study come particularly close to the mark. The first is that every creative person achieved a significant degree of mastery over their domain of work. So a good background in architecture — or a good working relationship with an architect — might be essential for the design work at hand. The second observation is that every creator referred back to their own childhood learning and demonstrated an ability to bring a fresh, childlike mind to their work.

By now such statements should raise red flags for us: here's that word *mastery* again, only here it's presented in an extremely positive way. And here again is the *childlike* quality which we just discussed in the context of ritual and make-believe — the ability to suspend consensus reality and enter completely into a fantastic or magical dimension. We are returning to the dance of mastery and mystery, with some indication that, in proper balance, the two forces work well together. Yet another red flag goes up when we visit the work of Csikszentmihalyi, who says that optimal experience, which certainly includes creativity, is a function of the state of consciousness which he labels "flow." Linking creativity to our state of consciousness is an extremely hopeful and positive proposition, and one which resonates well with the themes we have just discussed. Although we have limited control over present or future circumstances, and none at all over the past, our state of mind is one of the few things on which we can have a direct and demonstrable impact.

STATES OF CONSCIOUSNESS AND THE TRANSPERSONAL EXPERIENCE

Chapter Five

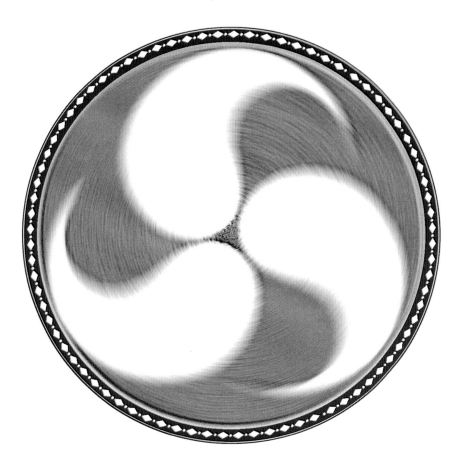

As two is the number of the opposites, and four is the number of Nature, three is of the divine — the trinity found throughout world cultures as Brahma-Vishnu-Shiva; Father, Son and Holy Ghost; upper-, middle- and lower-worlds. The Japanese *tomoye* is the same as the Celtic *triskelion* or the three-lobed windows found in Gothic cathedrals. Contemplating this image sets up a more integrative energy than that of the Yin-Yang.

We have touched on the fact that creativity may be linked to states of mind, and we have described a creative process whereby the solid ego dissolves and we are able to journey *transpersonally* (beyond ourselves) into the archetypal realm. To be able to enter such non-ordinary states of mind at will is the cornerstone of the "technologies of the sacred" and a key tool of Archetype Design.

Without exception, non-ordinary states of consciousness are the key to the realms of creativity and transformation which we seek to explore. So we need to become conversant with these states, which may be categorized as follows:

1. Meditative states
2. States of Flow
3. Ecstatic and trance states
4. Dream states (discussed in the following chapter)

We refer to these states as *non-ordinary* instead of altered to emphasize that these are natural and wholesome conditions which may be attained without mind-altering substances. All of us are perfectly familiar with at least a few non-ordinary states. We all have dreams and reveries, we all enjoy moments of rapture, and surely we've all had the "aha!" experience in response to nature, art, or sudden insight. And for anyone who remains skeptical about the power of states of mind, just think about falling in love, when the slightest glance or kiss is enough to turn the world upside down.

Though far from new in the world traditions, non-ordinary states may appear frightening at first. This is because the wide spectrum of potential states of mind has for centuries been compressed by religious dogma and a materialist culture to a sadly narrow range of sanctioned experience. Conformity and productivity are well-rewarded, while non-ordinary states are generally undervalued and are often discredited, banished, and even pathologized. This began for every one of us when as children we were admonished for daydreaming and praised for our accomplishments. So the work at hand is to become familiar with non-ordinary states, to make them more accessible, and to strip them of the overlays of fear and judgment in order to freshly experience them and the valuable opportunities they offer.

In so doing we are connecting with traditions which have existed since the earliest evidence of ritual or spiritual practice — 40,000 years ago or more. From the shamans to the mystics, from the Eleusinian mysteries to the founding vision of all the major religions, non-ordinary states of consciousness have been the medium for the deepest human experience. As we remarked before, each of us in our own childhoods surely spent countless hours immersed in distant realms of make-believe and creative fantasy. And so, far from breaking new ground, as we explore non-ordinary states of consciousness we are simply rediscovering territory which our ancestors and even we as children have already trod.

At the outset we must distinguish between wholesome and unwholesome states of mind. Intoxication, extreme rage, paranoia and some psychotic states for the most part lack the critical healing element. Related to these are powerful but destructive states of mind associated with illicit experiences such as violence, sexual extremes, and substance abuse. All of these states are tremendously powerful, and so it comes as no surprise that out of fear of the unwholesome states *all* non-ordinary states have been banished, including the wholesome ones. Not only have the powerful contents of the unconscious been suppressed for ages in favor of stability, but so have the states of mind which make the unconscious accessible.

When we venture into the little-known waters of non-ordinary states, it is normal to experience this ancestral fear. And so it is wise to begin with soft and gentle experiences which are generally pleasant and encouraging. As we discover the value of such journeying and build trust in our inner guide, we will be better prepared to encounter the darker and wilder aspects of ourselves. In time, and to the extent that we are willing to let go of control, we can access the truly extraordinary states of mind which facilitate deeper inner journeys.

Meditative States

While there are many schools and styles of meditation to be found in the world traditions, here the emphasis is on those which stabilize the mind and bring us into the present moment. Achieving enlightenment, acquiring yogic powers, or attaining transcendent states is, at least initially, far less important than simply becoming mindful.

Bearing the primal element of fire, hearth is perhaps the most powerful example of archetype in architecture. The fireplace above is as ceremonial as it is inviting, while the detailing of the kitchen range below subtly highlights the sacredness of food and its preparation.

The entrance to this house states unambiguously the owners' "built myth"
of love and affirmation.

The same entrance features
a gracious outdoor room
which welcomes the visitor
and provides a wonderful
transition from the speedy
and mechanized energy
of the car.

This entrance offers a different symbolic experience to the visitor who passes between the two eaglewing figures towards the single door and roundtop window behind.

If all our homes were even ten percent solar-efficient, the cumulative impact would be enormous. This rammed-earth house demonstrates that solar can indeed be beautiful.

The archetypes of nature as found in the canyon country inspired the buttresses, archways and sinuous walls which make these two homes feel as if they grew from the earth herself.

Meditative states are in many ways the foundation of all the other non-ordinary states, because they provide the equilibrium and stability of mind which allow us to journey successfully. Meditation is essentially a discipline which trains the mind to be fully focused on whatever experience is arising at this very moment. Many methods begin by sitting still and maintaining careful attention to the breath until, over many sessions, a basic level of concentration is established. Then, quite gradually, one can broaden the scope of awareness to include other experiences such as physical sensations, thoughts, and feelings. With practice one's concentration deepens, and with concentration comes tranquility. Thus we develop a calm and reflective state which provides an ideal backdrop against which other states of mind may be distinguished. Physiologically, meditation typically produces relaxation and a calming of pulse, breath rate, and blood pressure.

Countless experiences and subtle states of mind may arise within this basic meditative awareness. Sensations of intense pleasure and pain will present themselves. The mind will tend to seesaw between restlessness and tranquility. Thoughts will come and go, attended by emotions of fear, anger and joy. At times intense energy may surge through the body, accompanied by rushes of emotion. Profound insight into ourselves and into the nature of life may spontaneously occur, often followed by deep rapture or serenity. Creative insight may arise pertaining to one's interests and work. (Naturally this can include architecture – and so meditation can contribute directly to our work, particularly in the advanced stages of practice).

With practice, meditation cultivates a stable "center" of basic awareness which allows us to receive and to process any arising experience with equanimity. The need to grasp pleasant experiences and push away the unpleasant ones diminishes. Above all, meditation teaches us to let go and fearlessly allow the endless display of sensations, thoughts, and mind states to come and go freely. A sense of self begins to arise which surpasses the body and the ego, pointing to an ultimate identity which transcends the waves of experience, yet also includes them. Paradoxically, the expanded self may be experienced as no-self, or perhaps as identification with all selves. We are now well prepared to journey more actively – and indeed, some advanced forms of meditation do serve to dissolve the ego and open the doors to transpersonal experience.

Other types of meditation feature visualization and inner journeying. Tibetan Buddhists, for example, engage in elaborate visualizations which include the entire pantheon of gentle and wrathful deities as well as the mandalas which Jung recognized as transformative symbols. Other guided meditations common to psychotherapy and spiritual practice also rely on imagery to move energy and emotion. Quite aside from the specific goals of such meditations, the simple ability to visualize has obvious advantages for design work: with practice it is possible to imagine every detail of a proposed house and viscerally experience the energy of a design. Cultivating this skill helps with both the inner journey and the design process.

Practices such as hatha yoga, *tai chi* and *chi qong* incorporate bodily postures and movement to induce a healing flow of energy in the body as well as promote meditative awareness. What is added here is an intensified body awareness, a powerful counterweight to the mental focus so dominant in our culture. The importance of *body awareness* or *body wisdom* should not be overlooked. As we will see, the experience of architecture is substantially *kinesthetic* – that is, it is through the movement of the body through space that we derive a spatial experience. The very fact that we report afterwards how the space "feels" suggests an intimate link between body wisdom and our emotional or feeling center.

Of the countless forms of meditation available, we will explore three techniques which are particularly relevant to our work in creativity and transformation. *Vipassana* is a fundamental Buddhist practice which develops mindfulness and insight. The Seven Chakra breath meditation in Appendix B generates energy, articulates levels of consciousness, and fosters awareness of energy in the body. The Cosmic Tree meditation given in Chapter Six grounds us in the shamanic view of lower- and upperworld. All three involve a shift to a non-ordinary state of consciousness, and all three provide experiential learning which brings to life the theory of Part One.

Vipassana Meditation

Of the countless forms of meditation available, *vipassana* is perhaps the best suited for developing the primary tool of mindfulness. Conveniently, it is also the most widely practiced meditation technique in this country, with weekly sitting groups active in many cities. Numerous resources are available to follow up this beginning introduction to vipassana.

The Pali word vipassana is usually translated as *insight*, reflecting the basic Buddhist premise that if we develop deep and unwavering mindfulness we will be able to see into the nature of existence, enabling us to live in a wise and compassionate way. In its advanced stages vipassana actually deals with very subtle non-ordinary states of consciousness as well as transpersonal phenomena. The beginning instructions which follow, however, have a more limited goal of cultivating the fundamentals of basic awareness and equanimity.

Find a place where you can sit undisturbed for at least fifteen minutes, preferably a spot which is set aside as your sacred space. You will need a soft mat and a meditation pillow or bench, or if you prefer, a firm chair. All that is important is that you be able to sit in a comfortable and stable way with the back as straight as possible.

Begin by assuming your sitting posture and doing a quick body scan, making any necessary adjustments and letting go of obvious tension. In particular, let go of tightness in the neck, jaws, tongue, and eyes. Allow your weight to sink towards the floor, and become aware of the contact between your body and the pillow or chair. Last, bring your awareness to the belly and allow it to loosen and relax.

Now become aware of the sensations in the abdomen created by the breath as it rises and falls. (If you prefer, you can focus on the chest or the nostrils). This will be your primary object of meditation for the entire session. Simply watch the physical sensations of breathing. It may be helpful to mentally repeat "rising, falling" as the belly rises with the inbreath and falls on the outbreath. If you find your attention wandering, just return gently to the breath. This is the complete instruction for the early sessions, and if you practice daily for at least fifteen minutes, you will find your concentration improving in a matter of days.

All subsequent steps in vipassana build on the foundation of steadfastly observing the breath. When concentration has been established, it is possible to gently extend your attention to other phenomena which appear in the field of awareness. For example, if you become aware of physical sensations such as itching of the skin or throbbing of the muscles and joints, simply note them briefly as "itching, itching" or "throbbing, throbbing," and then bring your awareness back to the breath. Similarly with thoughts: "thinking, thinking" or "planning, planning." Emotions may be labeled as "anger, anger" or "sadness, sadness." There is no need to analyze – just note thoughts, feelings or sensations, and then return to the breath.

With continued practice concentration deepens, and with it comes tranquility as sensations and thoughts lose their ability to sway us. Pain is revealed as just a bundle of sensations which we can allow to go on without being shaken; thoughts come and go like clouds in the sky without our having to think them; emotions rise and fall like ocean waves, but we learn to identify with the vastness of the ocean. We begin to experience peace of mind and a calm, stable awareness.

The meditative experience includes a right-brain shift, and with it an opening of our feeling and intuitive faculties. Powerful states of rapture, creativity and insight arise as the formerly solid structures of our mind begin to release. Body awareness is greatly enhanced: we become quite sensitized to energy movements in the body as well as to energy and emotion in the environment, which of course includes people, building sites, and buildings.

States of Flow

Flow is a very general term for peak experiences and elevated states associated with daily *activities* rather than inward-oriented practices. Whereas in meditation the explicit intention is to shape consciousness, in many cases of flow the focus is actually on goal-oriented activity, with the mind state arising as a by-product or secondary feature.

Csikszentmihayli, who coined the term *flow*, details many variations of the state in his book by that title. States of flow generally reflect a condition of absorption which comes from applying intense concentration and appropriate skills to concrete goals such as work or recreational activities. Oft-mentioned activities include longdistance running, music, writing, and gardening. Here, intention is the tool which orders information, focuses attention, and hence controls consciousness.

The results are reported to be feelings of effortless control, peak performance, satisfaction, creativity, and relative freedom from the constraints of time and self-consciousness. While flow may not provide reliable access to the very deep levels of creativity we seek in Archetype Design, it most certainly describes an optimal state for the physical and interpersonal work of designing, drafting, and building.

Right Brain States

Research in recent decades has provided us with the model of the bi-cameral or two-sided brain which has very great relevance to both our journey and our design work. This model says that the two halves of the brain have very different characteristics. The left-brain mediates logic, speech, linear thought, our sense of time, and the right side of the body. It is rational, conceptual, masculine. By contrast, the right-brain operates as intuitive, spatial, and irrational. It is atemporal and deals in (guess what!) images and emotion. It directs the left side of the body and it is clearly feminine.

Obviously it is the *right-brain* which we want to utilize most on our journey within as well as in our design work. We could liken the left-brain to the engineer or guardian of function, while the right-brain is the artist or visionary. In Archetype Design we focus almost entirely on the visionary side (which of course has been under-utilized in our culture), knowing that we will return to the engineer at the proper time.

An interesting finding has been that left- and right-brain dominance is an either/or proposition: for the most part we can function in just one side at a time. In particular, the right brain comes into its own only when the left brain and its male dominance bows out. In the language of our Journey, it is only when the ego-mind of judgment and logic has been dissolved that the intuitive and image-oriented faculties can truly flower.

In *Drawing on the Right Side of the Brain*, Betty Edwards articulates a method for creating right-brain shift through drawing. Her technique, which is currently in use in some architecture schools, is excellent for both the inner journey and the design process. The shift to the intuitive and image-oriented mind is accomplished by relinquishing the critical judging mind, by focusing on the hand-eye process rather than on the product, and by becoming absorbed in the details of the image itself. Very quickly one becomes aware of the right-brain shift: the mind shifts out of time, out of linear thought, into the body, and into a relaxed and creative state. With practice, one learns to move in and out of this state more or less at will.

Results include relaxation, transcendence of time, grounding in the body, emotional acuity, and a greatly enhanced ability to perceive detail and spatial relationships.

Trance and Ecstasy

The states we have reviewed thus far all involve a dynamic interplay between concentration and relaxation. A certain alert awareness is necessary — but too much can turn into restlessness. Relaxation and letting go is equally essential — but here an excess invites slackness. All these states feature relatively subtle departures from the ordinary, and for the most part they are compatible with the demands of everyday situations.

By contrast, the states of trance and ecstasy are quite removed from the ordinary waking state, invariably entailing a marked but temporary dissolution of the ego-mind. Far more emotional and excitatory, they are the states which provide the inner journeys we seek in Archetype Design.

Trance refers to states which are associated with deep concentration and inner journey. They have a dreamlike quality of absorption, whereas *ecstasy* is more of an expansive and energized outward movement towards transcendence or identifications beyond the usual sense of self. Trance is more likely to result from deep meditation or shamanic journey, while ecstasy might come from dance, drumming, or devotional practices. There are no hard and fast distinctions between trance and ecstasy — in fact, consciousness research is just beginning to differentiate between these states and their variations. Common experiences include the sensation of being out-of-body, beyond pain, beyond time, and beyond self, with the sense of being catapulted out of equilibrium *(ex-stasis)* and into intense rapture. Visions, inner sound, and spontaneous insight are frequent. The physiological results may be dramatic, from a vastly increased rate of heart and breath to the opposite extreme, when the breath actually stops and heart rate slows markedly.

Such powerful states are usually the result of focused spiritual practices. Several, including meditation, shamanic journey, and Holotropic Breathwork, are part of our workshops. Other techniques include ecstatic drumming and dancing, *pranayama* (yogic breathing), fasting, devotional practices, and the use of psychotropic plants. Such practices are found worldwide and vary by culture, and even within a culture experiences differ greatly from individual to individual. But the common thread is a transcendence of personal identifications and ego, and a journey into the transpersonal realm which lies beyond.

Though such states and transformative experiences may seem hopelessly beyond the reach of the newcomer, in practice they are rather easily accessed. Because non-ordinary states are as natural to us as daydreaming, there is no reason for anyone to shy away from this work thinking they are not capable of it. Quite the contrary: early experiences tend to be particularly vivid and transformative as reserves of pent-up energy are finally released and expressed.

The Transpersonal Experience

The experiences resulting from non-ordinary states have challenged the ability of western psychology to account for them and have helped give birth to the transpersonal movement, which for two decades has attempted to integrate the insights of the world's spiritual traditions with western psychology and current consciousness research. Archetype Design has very definitely arisen in the context of this movement as described by one of its pioneers, Stan Grof:

> *"Transpersonal experiences can be defined as experiential expansion or extension of consciousness beyond the usual boundaries of the body-ego and beyond the limitations of time and space. They cover an extremely wide range of phenomena which occur on different levels of reality; in a sense, the entire spectrum of transpersonal experiences is commensurate with existence itself."*
> — Stanislav Grof, *The Adventure of Self-Discovery*, p.38

The first contribution of transpersonal psychology has been to take inventory of the range of human experience to which Grof refers, embracing many which western science has previously dismissed as archaic, delusional, or even pathological. These include dreams, archetypal encounters, near-death experiences, shamanic journeys, mystical visions, psychedelic sessions, psychic phenomena, past-life memories, traumatic episodes and certain psychotic states. In *The Adventure of Self-Discovery* and *The Holotropic Mind*, Grof presents a comprehensive overview of such experiences, many of them made possible by non-ordinary states of consciousness and in particular by his technique of Holotropic Breathwork.

Next, the transpersonal movement has integrated the perennial philosophy of mankind as encoded in the worldwide spiritual traditions. For example, the maps of consciousness provided by Hindu and Buddhist meditators, longtime connoisseurs of the inner journey, have been incorporated (see Vaughan & Walsh). Also included is the shamanic cosmology of journey into the lower- and upperworlds for insight and healing. As a result a new model has emerged to account for our experience and provide at least the beginning of a cartography for the Journey. An example is the spectrum of consciousness developed by Ken Wilber in his many books.

These developments have been augmented by the new physics, by ongoing consciousness research, and most recently by the urgent need for a worldview of sustainability. The overall result is a significant revision to western psychology. Though this is very much of an ongoing process, to date the emerging transpersonal model features:

1. *A more highly differentiated map of consciousness and of the different levels of reality.* A cartography of consciousness is beginning to take shape, pairing the growing list of validated experiences with maps of mind states. However, it is clear that transpersonal experience is complex and multi-dimensional. Being by definition beyond the usual limitations of time and space, such experience does not easily yield to the desire of the rational mind to quantify and localize. Like attempts to describe quantum particles, a transpersonal cartography is likely to have the character of holography, of probabilities, or of "tendencies to exist." *Most important* is the simple fact that the methods of systematic self-exploration and experiential confirmation are now being validated and given a meaningful frame of reference.

2. *A broader and more flexible understanding of the collective unconscious, the archetypes, and archetypal systems.* The Jungian view is up for review in the light of the increased availability of transpersonal experiences in recent decades. For example, whereas Jung lumped superconsciousness together with the unconscious, actual experience suggests that the two are quite distinct. Much of the collective unconscious pertains to the pre-personal level, which resembles the chthonic lowerworld of early cosmologies and pertains to instincts, patterns of survival, racial and ancestral memories, and our phylogenetic heritage. Certain mythological and nature archetypes are associated with this domain. By contrast, anima, animus, persona and shadow are archetypes of the personal level — templates for the dynamics of personality. When we arrive at the transpersonal or spiritual level we find divine messengers, deity archetypes and a few Jungian archetypes such as Wise Woman. This is the upperworld domain of superconsciousness, which has a transcendent aspect distinct from the pre-personal. However, certain archetypes including Hero and Trickster operate at more than one level, while the symbolized archetypes of transformation (the universal laws of nature) operate at all three. The tableau is exceedingly complex, and it is made all the more so by the way non-ordinary states experientially link the unconscious and the superconscious levels, often providing access to both realms in the same session. This ability to move freely between levels definitely invites confusion, and thus distinguishing the various levels becomes a matter of practice over time. It must be emphasized, however, that knowing the roadmap is not nearly as important as travelling the road — moreover, our roadmap is constantly developing. Nevertheless, it may be useful to refer to Figure I, which summarizes this description in graphic form.

An intriguing phenomenon of the past several years is the widespread emergence into popular culture of archetypal symbols such as spirals, kokopellis, serpent figures, and variations of the solar disc. Though easy to dismiss as a media-driven trend, this emergence could equally well signal an upswell of material from the collective unconscious, coming at a time when humanity as a whole badly needs to reconnect with the universal, healing energies which these symbols represent. Equally significant is the degree to which crossovers are being reported between archetypal systems. Whereas archetypal experiences were formerly limited to the domain of one's own culture, it now appears that access is increasingly available to all corners of the collective unconscious. This is in direct parallel to the shrinking

The Journey

Trans-Personal
Upperworld

· *Beyond Body & Ego*
· *Transcendence*

Deity Archetypes
Wise Old Man & Woman
Trickster
Hero

Personal
Middleworld

· *Personality*
· *Relationships*

Persona
Shadow
Anima
Animas

Pre-Personal
Lowerworld

· *Biology*
· *Phylogenetic/Racial/Ancestral*

Power Animals
Nature Spirits
Mythological Figures

Great Mother

Universal Symbols of Transformation
Timeless Laws of Nature

Lowerworld & Upperworld Interpenetrate Through World Tree

and interconnecting of the outer world, suggesting that we may be seeing the beginning of a new global archetypology. Today a vast menu of archetypal sources is at our disposal, each offering its distinct insights and gifts. Jungian psychology continues to excel at the level of personality, where the dynamics of the persona, shadow, anima and animus archetypes in particular provide a window into human interactions. The archetypes of Tibetan Buddhism offer access to a specialized tradition of spiritual transformation (particularly as regards death), while those of indigenous cultures can effectively ground us in ways of healing and of connecting with the earth. The *chakra* system is a wonderful tool for developing our multi-leveled spiritual dimensions, while the East Asian meridian system of medicine provides a framework for energy flow and healing. Other archetypal systems include astrology, numerology, and the traditional Chinese worldview of which *feng shui* is a part. We can never predict what archetype or archetypal system we will encounter — the inner healer takes us where it will — but if we proceed with trust and fully receive whatever experience arises, then healing and transformation can occur spontaneously in every case. Over time we have the opportunity to weave our experiences into a new cosmology.

3. *A vision of a journey towards wholeness which is at once spiritual, social, and ecological.* The model of the Sacred Journey seems to fit the spirit of our age at the same time that it embraces and organizes our actual experience. It resembles the Hindu concept of *lila*, which says that all of creation is but an infinite play of the Divine which simply wishes to experience itself. Beginning with the present moment, the Journey to the Self moves first through the terrain of our biography and then passes through successively more collective levels of both pre- and transpersonal experience, during which all unresolved conflicts and wounds are healed. This view is actually quite similar to the Mahayana Buddhist goal of developing perfect compassion for all beings — the "beings" in this case being identical with the infinite aspects of ourselves. In our time, the resurgent awareness that we are separate from neither our global society nor the biosphere adds a special and urgent quality to the work. As a species, we can no longer afford the luxury of walking our spiritual path in isolation from the needs of the world around us.

A further comment is in order here, having to do with the pitfalls as well as the advantages of transpersonal work. Transpersonal experience can unearth tremendously rich material — visions and archetypal encounters can transform us, as well as provide us with powerful images to think and talk about. Yet the very experiences which fuel the creative journey can become obstacles if the ego-mind attaches to them and we become infatuated with experience itself. Like the Buddha who sat unflinching under the bodhi tree as the temptations of Mara passed before him, one must cultivate the ability to experience fully and let go at the same time. This is where a strong meditation practice is our greatest friend, helping us to avoid the traps of our own story line. The goal is not to collect the most dazzling set of journeys, nor even to become the most creative architect in town. While these might be welcome by-products, the real goal is to become whole, and that means going beyond any narrow focus on experiences.

The greatest value of transpersonal experiences is not the flashy display, but rather the simple opportunity to dwell for a period of time beyond body and ego. When one is in deep transpersonal states and can look back at the ego as from a mountaintop, it is absolutely clear that ego is an illusion consisting of nothing more than a swirl of desire, clinging, judgment, aversion, and fear — qualities which, though they do help us survive, doom us to live as limited and separate entities. Journeying beyond ego, we know ourselves to be ultimately free of those hindrances, and for as long as we spend in the transpersonal state, we have the opportunity to "rewire" ourselves and come into alignment with a different reality — one of compassion, wholeness, humor, and peace. This re-alignment can be enduring, and thus when we return to ordinary consciousness it simply may not possible to buy back into the cage of ego in the same way as before. Once we have known our true home of freedom, it is difficult to return to a lesser sense of self.

★★★★★

The transpersonal experience, shattering as it does our conventional notions of self, offers a rich and exciting expansion of consciousness. Within it, we enjoy the archetypal and creative encounters which will inform our house design. Yet this journey appears to be a never-ending one which sets off into unbelievably vast territory. In the context of our work, is it reasonable to narrow our focus to the elements which pertain to house design?

The dilemma is this: when we open the doors to the deepest creative realms for the purposes of design, we are also opening to the many other gifts and challenges which await us there. To a limited extent — and more consistently with practice — we can mount quick reconnaissance missions to obtain specific insight or information. It is also true that our intentions to produce healing design work will tend to attract the inner experiences we seek. But, for the most part, we will inevitably undergo transformation when we journey beyond the self for creative insight. To illustrate this, I offer my own experience from a Holotropic Breathwork session:

My experience developed very quickly, as I entered the session with an intense yearning to be reunited with my Self. Within minutes I felt a powerful surge of kundalini moving up my spine, stopping at the heart center. Pressure built up in my heart, which felt like it would burst at any second. I found myself praying "take me, please take me." Moments later my heart burst open, and my consciousness instantly exploded outward, seemingly filling the universe. For some minutes I had no awareness of myself as separate – there was only a complete and seamless One which was beyond even color and form. Soon however, I began to return. First the color gold appeared, and when my sense of separate self returned, I knew myself as vast and pure love. As thoughts arose and images and sounds of the panorama of existence began to pass before my awareness, I experienced myself as simply being a pure and loving heart, devoid of all judgment and grasping. The bliss was inexpressible as tears ran freely down my face and my breath all but stopped. I remained in this state for perhaps an hour. At one point I saw on my inner screen a dazzling pyramid – it was absolutely shimmering with a numinous iridescent purple at the base, capped with a golden light which radiated out like the sun itself. This was followed by a perfect pyramid-shaped mountain, also glowing but capped with snow like Fuji-san or Mount Shasta. There followed a sequence of mountain-like temples – Shiva temples with lingam spires, Shakti temples with breastlike domes, and multi-tiered stupas. So great was my bliss that these images passed almost unnoticed. Only later did I realize that these were architectural representations of archetypal energies, and that in transcending my self and merging with the One I had contacted the Source of sacred architecture and The Creative itself. Thus was Archetype Design born.

Since this seminal experience (which, readers might be encouraged to know, was in my second breathwork session), my journeys have displayed a characteristic intertwining of my spiritual path and my professional life as a designer — in truth, there seems to be no separating the two. Frequently the first part of a session will feature spiritual or emotional healing — for example, I might be dealing with a bodily pain associated with emotional pain in a relationship, and both might be linked to a wound from the distant past. Resolution and healing come as I open to the pain and simply breathe through it. Journeying on, I am likely to have an archetypal encounter — quite possibly with a figure who is related to the emotional theme I have just experienced, and who furthers the healing at a deeper level. Sooner or later I am likely to see something architectural: perhaps an insight about music and architecture, or possibly an experience of a transformational arched doorway, complete with all of the emotion and energy which the image carries. In this way I am healed and transformed at the same time that the Creative flows through me. For me this is as it should be: the gifts of the spirit flowing into and informing design.

THE SHAMANIC JOURNEY

Chapter Six

The ancient cosmology is depicted as the Cosmic Tree. The visible branches of the Upperworld are mirrored by the vast roots of the Lowerworld. They are connected by the central trunk, the *axis mundi* of mythology, which also passes through our Middleworld and is the means of passage between all three.

Shamanism is at once the oldest spiritual tradition in the world and the newest one to hit the new age magazines and retreat centers of the United States and Europe. Its enormous appeal is understandable in view of a heightened interest in the environment and by the allure of any sort of spiritual attainment which is perceived to go hand-in-hand with a return to nature. And indeed, shamanism does foster a deep attunement to the earth and to the very old "technologies of the sacred" which have been abandoned in the course of the modern empirical rush. For our purposes, shamanic journey has a dual potential: it can open the door to visionary and archetypal experiences which contribute to house design, and it can vitalize our sense of the Sacred Journey.

However, it is advisable to distinguish traditional shamanism from the current fad, because the new age circuit is home to more than a few self-styled shamans who are hanging out their shingles on the strength of enthusiasm and the barest bit of training. This is quite a different matter from traditional shamanic initiation. Well-documented accounts describe the initiate actually being seized by the spirits and pulled into other realms, typically undergoing months of illness or madness and even coming close to death before beginning the return to a functional role in society (Eliade, pp.33-66). Alternatively, formal initiation and years of training at the hands of a master shaman are required to generate shamanic awareness, stabilize it, and give it productive expression. Rigorous training in the use of plant medicines and other healing techniques is frequently part of the instruction. In many cultures the shamanic descent is considered to be quite dangerous, with some instances of the shaman never returning from the journey. This is a depth of experience to which few of us aspire, and one which the typical introductory workshop is not likely to provide. Nor does the work contemplated in Archetype Design approach this level of commitment.

Shamanic journey, as we speak of it here, is a method of separating one's consciousness from the body in order to gain access to other dimensions for the purpose of information or healing. This is generally a highly intentional act which is focused on a specific purpose, and to the extent that the journey is colored by intention, it is not necessarily a purely transpersonal experience. But, though vestiges of planning mind or thinking mind may remain, this by no means diminishes the potential of shamanic journey for contributing to our creative quest.

The Shamanic Worldview

The cosmology of the ancients was rooted in the simplest facts of living between the earth below and the sky above — *an architecture of the outer world which appears to be mirrored in the psyche as the basic architecture of our inner nature.* This structure survives in the Judeo-Christian notion of heaven above and hell below, and it endures in the transpersonal view of the pre-personal, personal and transpersonal levels of the psyche. Perry describes this ancient outlook as follows:

> *"Man's everyday life is bounded by a spiritual world above and a chthonic world below, the former associated with the Father, the latter with the Mother...above is the sky world from which comes order and the righteousness that puts order into effect, the organizing activity of ideals and of possibilities of form; this Father domain is characterized by the principals of clarity, illumination and rationality. Within the body of the Mother, the earth, is all of the paradox of the feminine: darkness and chaos are yet accompanied by the life-urge itself, which gives forth with profuse abundance in the raw. In her darkness is also death, yet in this case death is the source out of which arises renewed life. Below is her abyss, out of which emerges the raw substance of cosmos, needing the molding hand of creativeness from the masculine above to give it form and proportion and structure."*

— John Perry, *Lord of the Four Quarters*, p. 27

This imprint surfaces frequently in journeys and dreams as images of the earth surrounded by water and capped with the dome of the sky. Caves, grottos, canyons and tunnels variously represent journeys into the interior of the Mother, while the ascent to the peaks or to the sky itself are journeys to the Father realm. The two realms clearly have entirely different characteristics, which we will articulate further as we learn how shamanic journey works. Both realms are within us, and both have a collective nature — that is, at deep levels untinged by culture, everyone shares the same lowerworld and the same upperworld and is connected by them.

Shamanic Journey

Shamanism takes the ancient cosmology as its basic roadmap. All journeys start from this, the middleworld of everyday reality, and for the most part are directed to the lower- or upperworlds. Upperworld journeys might be to obtain spiritual insight and higher truth, while lowerworld journeys would more likely be for physical or emotional healing. Middleworld journeys, while infrequent, are typically made for ordinary information such as avoiding danger, locating prey, or surveilling enemies. (For example, remote viewing is a type of middleworld journey). Whatever the destination, a shift of consciousness takes place. The techniques for this shift vary: drumming, singing, and dancing are most common, but psychotropic plant medicines such as ayahuasca or psilicybin are sometimes ingested. In all cases the shaman relies on assistance from ancestral spirits, allies or power animals which inhabit such realms. (Eliade, pp. 67-109).

Traditional shamanism is as demanding a path as it is an ancient one, and has its origins in a vivid mythological understanding of the world. Whereas an indigenous person might feel she was literally descending into another world, we might be inclined to interpret the journey as one into nether regions of our own psyche. Rather than view power animals as autonomous entities, we might see them as personifications of our own psychic energies. So, as with any ancient system we encounter, we may adapt shamanic practices to our own time and our own path. Few of us are going to set forth to the rainforest in search of shamanic initiation, nor will everyone feel quite comfortable with drumming, dancing, plant medicines and power animals. Furthermore, whereas shamanism traditionally offered the best available means of healing, directing the hunt, or of dealing with enemies, it is valid to ask if it retains any relevance in a world of modern medicine, internet investing and global politics.

However, stripped of cultural trappings, shamanism is simply a different technique for gaining access to other planes of existence through non-ordinary states of consciousness. In this way it is closely related to dream experiences, Holotropic Breathwork, or spontaneous expressions of rapture or insight. Certainly our experiences as members of a technological culture are likely to be quite different from those of indigenous people. A contemporary American, for example, is not likely to visit the same transpersonal realms as a rainforest tribesman. It is far more likely that we will visit territory which relates to our own archetypology and belief systems, encountering archetypal figures, nature spirits, mystical visions, or unresolved sequences from our past.

The distinguishing characteristic of shamanic journey is that it is highly intentional: whereas in Holotropic Breathwork we are trained to receive whatever images and emotions our inner healer sends us, the shaman journeys for a quite specific purpose such as healing, information, or creative vision. Thus we have at our disposal a very different tool which can be used specifically for both architectural and transformational purposes. The basic sequence is as follows: first, we enter an altered state; second, we project our consciousness to a place where the information or inspiration is to be found; third, we return with the prize. Though at first glance the process looks like active imagination or free association, in fact the altered state makes a significant difference. Here we won't be imagining or fantasizing anything — we'll actually go there. We will be entering an altered state and enlisting the aid of a power animal to take us to a region of the psyche where answers await us.

Which region of the psyche we visit is up to us — or, we can let our power animal be the guide. Perhaps a word about power animals would be helpful at this point. Some practitioners take their power animals to be objectively real (like an ally in the domain of spirit, quite separate from one's own consciousness) while others accept them as representations of aspects of the psyche (a part of our own minds, conveniently projected as an animal). In truth, this distinction is functionally unimportant, because ultimately the power animal is simply a device to help us let go of willfulness and allow the inner guide to lead. Call it innate intelligence, call it grace, call it what you please — surrender and letting go are an integral part of the equation. Of course, such relinquishing of control is easier said than done, which is why we use the power animal — it simply works.

Michael Harner's *The Way of the Shaman* offers a good introduction to shamanic journey. Drumming tapes are available to support the work, as are Harner-style groups in many locations across the United States. First, using repetitive drumming to induce the shamanic trance, the novice learns to journey into the lowerworld and to return. The next step is to invoke or "dance in" one's power animal, which prepares the initiate to journey to the lowerworld for the benefit of others: for example, to bring back their power animals to heal them, or to retrieve dissociated or lost parts of the soul.

There are countless variations on this technique, and over time every practitioner will develop his or her own methods. With experience it is quite possible to journey without the trappings of drums and power animals.
In Archetype Design we explore only the beginning levels of shamanic journey, and we stay with the basic forms. Thus drumming is used to induce the non-ordinary state of consciousness, and in the very first session the participant contacts his or her power animal. In the second session the participant sets an intention — for example, to obtain insight on the choice of a building site — and journeys inside to meet the power animal. The power animal is asked to take the traveler to a place where the information is to be found, and the journey begins. The answer may be in the lowerworld of primordial energy and natural forms, or it could be in the upperworld realm of spiritual knowledge, higher truth, and sacred geometry. In either case, the information is felt or seen, and the traveler returns to the ordinary state of consciousness bearing the desired insight. Ten to twenty minutes is sufficient for the entire process.

The following is an account of one such journey:

As the session began I formed the simple intention of journeying to the upperworld for any architectural insight which might present itself. I began by going to my place of power, a spot by a stream with mountains on one side and a deep canyon on the other. There I called Turtle, and asked her to take me on this journey. Presently Turtle rose skyward with me in tow. We slipped into a fold in the clouds and instantly passed beyond the atmosphere into a realm of light. Here, traced in lines of light, was a holographic image of a kiva-like round room with a flat roof. There was a pyramid skylight in the center, and I saw that the four diagonal lines of the pyramid, if they were fully extended, joined the walls at exactly ground level. Thus, although only the skylight section of the pyramid was actually constructed, the room carried the energy of the entire pyramid. At ground level the energy was of a square within a circle, but the energy rose higher and higher in more concentrated form until it cleared the roof level, reached one-pointedness at the peak of the pyramid, and was projected skyward. This was an answer to a problem I had been wrestling with: while previously I had seen the symbolic potential of a pyramid skylight, now I could experience the energetic level underlying the symbol. I could actually feel the energy created by these architectural forms! The session lasted

about fifteen minutes, and afterwards it was easy to sketch the vivid images I had seen. I don't think I would ever have stumbled on these solutions by imagination or conventional problem-solving. (This journey is illustrated in Chapter Twelve).

Quite aside from the immediate insight they provide, journeys of this sort open the door to our inherent potential for creative and transformative breakthroughs. Coming as we do from an aggressive culture of planners and achievers, it is a welcome relief to relax into a source of energy and insight which flows effortlessly from within. Moreover such information, since it is not tarnished by the exertions of the thinking mind, has a special capacity to challenge and stretch our awareness. Lowerworld experiences tend to ground us in elemental and nurturing energies of the earth, the four directions, the seasons, and the feminine. Upperworld journeys attune us to the heavens, to spiritual insight, to truth and beauty. Taken together, these influences help us to assume a balanced and healing place here in the middleworld between earth and sky.

Eventually our homes can reflect this same balance. We might build sunlit music rooms or art studios where we reach for the illumination of the skyworld, whereas bedrooms, dens and meditation spaces seek to delve into the mystery of the Mother. Upper and lower levels of a house can powerfully reinforce these themes, as can the skillful use of passageways and transitions. Choices of materials, colors and textures and placement of artwork can also develop this scheme. Very likely the kitchen, dining room and living spaces will have a more middleworld quality, though elements such as skylights, fireplaces, plants, and fountains might let the other worlds speak as well.

Of course, we already gravitate instinctively to some of these elements, which is really a confirmation of the appropriateness of an archetypal approach to design. As long as we have bodies, we are likely to think of the earth as Mother Nature and the heavens as the realm of the gods — and if our buildings reflect this fundamental structure, then we are likely to feel at home in them. And when, in addition, we have arrived at our design through *actual experience of the energies underlying the forms*, then the results will carry particular power and significance for us.

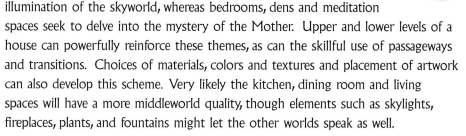

Cosmic Tree Meditation

Taking your seat as before, ground yourself in the awareness of the breath. Now visualize a big spreading tree – a real Grandmother of a tree – whose spreading branches are mirrored belowground by roots extending deeply into the earth. With every breath, sense the roots reaching down into the lowerworld, drawing water and nourishment from the soil. Let yourself experience whatever images or associations arise as your awareness penetrates the realm of the earth and the lowerworld, primal Mother. After a few minutes, pull your awareness slowly back up the roots and into the trunk of the Cosmic Tree, and then let your attention go to the branches above as they reach into the vast sky of the upperworld. Going out into the branches and twigs, feel the leaves turning to the sun for light and warmth. Feel the freshness of the breeze, the vibrancy of color, and the energy of photosynthesis as the canopy touches Father Sky.

After several minutes let the energy from the leaves sink gently back down into the trunk and into the roots, supplying the rest of the tree. Feel the opposing current of water and nutrients rising from the roots up to the branches. And now feel both the upward and downward flow simultaneously, maintaining for several minutes a balanced awareness of both the lowerworld and the upperworld.

This simple visualization is best practiced sitting directly on the earth herself, and it can be quite effective for creating both a visual and visceral sense of the shamanic worldview. Balance is the key to this meditation, and if you find that the visualization of either world comes much more easily, then it may be that you need to compensate through additional work with whichever is the less easily accessed realm. Very many people, for example, have a strong pull to the upperworld and hence tend to be spaced out – they can benefit from lowerworld grounding. In other words, the exercise can be a right-brain way of strengthening the earthy and feminine side of ourselves in order to balance the cultural bias towards the mental and masculine aspect. In this life, and in our homes as well, we need strong roots – or we might topple.

An alternative breathing practice for lower- and upperworld balance is as follows:

> Become grounded in the breath, and then breathe as if each inhalation were coming up through the feet and each exhalation were returning through the feet into the earth. After a few minutes, switch the direction so that each inbreath enters the crown and each outbreath returns out of the head toward the sky.

> Next, let the inbreath come from the earth and the outbreath go to the sky; then reverse the flow, with the inbreath coming from the sky and the exhalation going into the earth. Last, try to do both at once, visualizing a constant flow of energy through your body from earth and sky.

Practices such as these are extremely effective because they take what might otherwise be purely intellectual knowledge and ground it in experiential body wisdom. This point cannot be overemphasized. *Feeling is believing* — it's when we sense something in the body that we really understand its power. In many ways architecture is nothing more than taking vision and bringing it into physical form — so when we learn to actualize this process in our own bodies we are prepared to do the same thing at the drawing board.

THE "DREAM HOUSE" AND INTERIOR DESIGN

Chapter Seven

The familiar vortex of whirlpool, hurricane and tornado may be experienced within the psyche as a dynamic of transition from one state of consciousness to another. Shamans frequently descend to the Lowerworld by means of a vortex. The vortex is associated with the birth canal and the passage through death, both of which are characterized by light at the end of the tunnel.

In 1909 Carl Jung had a dream which forever changed our understanding of the psyche and added a new dimension to the term "dream house." In his dream he toured a house which, though unfamiliar, he knew to be his own. It had two levels aboveground and two below. The uppermost level was a salon which he found to be well lived-in, while the ground floor was from the sixteenth century and had an unoccupied air. A stone stairway descended to a cellar where the walls revealed old bricks from Roman times. Finally a trap door led down once again to a cave where pottery shards, bones and skulls lay strewn on the floor. (C.G. Jung, *Memories, Dreams, Reflections* p.158)

This was the famous dream from which Jung drew his concept of the collective unconscious. The upper story, he realized, was the conscious mind, while the ground floor was the personal unconscious. The belowground levels represented successively deeper levels of the collective unconscious.

From that time on, houses in dream interpretation have generally been regarded as representations of the self or of the personality. In other words, we can take it that *when we find ourselves dreaming of a house, our unconscious is presenting us with some issue or aspect of ourselves which it wants us to consider.*

Working With Dreams

The dream state is a naturally occuring, non-ordinary state of consciousness in which the thinking mind is temporarily on hold and we are wide open to experiences of the unconscious. Research has shown that everyone dreams several times each night, and so we know that dreams are constantly available to us. Throughout history people have looked to dreams for omens, healing, and spiritual guidance, trusting in the intelligence behind the dream as well as in our ability to derive meaning from it.

Since we are so open in the dream state, there is tremendous potential for directly accessing those dimensions of the psyche which we normally tune out. By their very nature, dreams speak to us not in linear or verbal terms, but in the right brain language of image, emotion, symbols and metaphor. The problem, however, is that most of us have lost touch with our dreams, and it requires practice to learn how to unravel their meaning. As a culture we are uncomfortable with uncertainty, and impatient with slow and gradual processes — yet that is precisely the usual shape of dreamwork.

Bookshelves are filled with works offering predominantly intellectual approaches to dreams, many calling for consistent and literal interpretations of dream symbols. For example, some theories insist that the kitchen *always* represents change because of the alchemical significance of fire. But what if the kitchen in a particular dream symbolizes healing — or nurturing? What if it amounts to nothing more than a rehash of the day's experience of being stuck in the kitchen all day? Who is to say, anyway? The problem with such literal systems is that they overlook an essential point which Jung himself knew quite well: what matters is *the significance of the dream to the dreamer*. Just as it is up to each of us to create our myth, it is primarily up to the individual to make sense of messages coming from the unconscious.

If we do turn to books or teachers for help with our dreams, it should be with the understanding that off-the-shelf interpretations are useful primarily to get us started. Any suggestions in this chapter are offered with this proviso: they are best used as tentative supports, to be quickly abandoned as the reader develops his or her own dream life.

Dreamwork begins with the simple intention to remember dreams and write them down *every day* in a dream journal. Even those who claim that they never dream find that with practice their recall quickly becomes vivid and detailed. Dream groups are also powerful tools for reinforcing dream recall. At the outset, it is quite enough to simply remember your dreams, paying special attention to the emotions experienced while dreaming and upon awakening. This continues the theme of *image and emotion* which we have already discussed.

Dreams can be divided into three categories corresponding to the shamanic worldview. The *lowerworld* is the primal, the unconscious, the feminine. Lowerworld dreams teem with the energies and forms of myth, archetype, animal powers, and the elements. The upperworld is the celestial dimension of spirit, angels, light, and of superconsciousness and psychic powers. Upperworld dreams feature divine messengers, angels, experiences of flight or healing, and journeys to peaks and sky realms. The middleworld is the intermediary dimension where we live every day, and its dreams feature everyday life situations and people. Each of these worlds has a distinct feeling or flavor, and thus a good first step in unraveling a dream is to recognize which type a dream fits.

At first, dream content may appear to be a flood of seemingly chaotic material. However, as we become more present with our dreams, focused or coherent stories and images appear more frequently. Some dreams stand out as especially vivid, portentous, or charged with emotion and meaning. Archetypal experiences in particular leave powerful impressions. When this occurs, *it is paramount to simply receive as fully and directly as possible the energy or emotion connected with the images.* At this point interpretation, which is a linear left-brain process, should be held back because there is nothing to be figured out mentally which cannot be apprehended far more directly and powerfully by the intuitive and feeling center. It can take hours or days for the body to process the energy of a powerful dream, during which time the intellect can actually be a hindrance.

Dream interpretation, then, has two aspects. One is right-brain and intuitive, and the other is left-brain and logical. It's the right-brain which is capable of reading the metaphors and symbols, and then the left-brain can proceed to grasp the logic and meaning of the entire sequence, translating dream information into real-life actions. Interpretation consists of an interplay between the two, with the intellect constantly checking in with intuition to make sure it hasn't strayed from the energetic and emotional core. Over time, dreamwork becomes easier as we develop a symbolic dream vocabulary and become familiar with the peculiar logic of dreams. Non-ordinary states of consciousness are seldom-appreciated tools for dream interpretation and offer the greatest potential for unlocking dream symbolism: after all, since the dream state is itself a non-ordinary one, it makes perfect sense that by entering a similar state of consciousness we could penetrate secrets which remain barred to the everyday mind. In this regard, dream groups can be enormously helpful to the extent that the group creates particular states of mind through meditation, drumming or journey.

To a limited extent dreams can be intentional — for some dreamers, it is possible to fall asleep with the plan of dreaming about a particular issue and to actually have the desired dream sequence. However, most of the time dreaming is a process of receiving whatever the psyche spontaneously serves up. Once again we will encounter diverse aspects of ourselves: dreams will unfailingly confront us with fears and anxieties, explicit sexual and relationship issues, and unresolved traumas — but not without also showing us how to heal them. On the happier side, dreams will highlight our higher gifts and abilities as well show us the way to realize our spiritual potential. In all of this, the help and support from an experienced dreamworker or group can be a great aid.

Dreams of houses present themselves quite often — usually far more frequently than dreams of other everyday objects such as cars, food or clothing. This fact alone suggests that houses have some special relationship to our psyches. Indeed, the very structure of "dream houses" corresponds to the structure of our bodies with foundations as the feet, windows as the eyes, and the roof as our head. Symbolically, upper stories, towers and rooftops represent the crown chakra and intellectual or superconscious qualities, while basements and dungeons are the lowerworld realms of the unconscious. Foundations are the foundations of our being. Stairways, especially spirals, are lower- or upperworld journeys, while tunnels and hallways are passageways of transformation. Bathrooms are places of water, which is emotion, life force, and the unconscious. The list goes on and on: windows are our outlook on the world and frequently refer to psychic or third eye vision; doorways are thresholds of transformation; skylights admit light from the upperworld, and fireplaces and stoves contain the alchemical fire of transformation.

The following example shows the kind of information our unconscious may be giving us through dreams of house. A woman dreamt she was refinishing her floor, pulling up nine successive layers of old material before reaching the lowest level. The layers of old flooring were rich and varied, and the bottom was a real surprise: whereas she expected to find a filthy and decayed slab, instead she discovered a wonderful wood surface which merely needed sanding and sealing to make a good finished floor. The feeling from the dream was positive — a mix of excitement and reassurance. With some help from her dream group she found the meaning: the dream related not only to her actual remodeling project at home, but also to the spiritual remodeling she was performing on herself. She learned that she needed to honor her varied and multi-layered past even as she worked to get down to the basis of her being. And she learned that her spiritual foundation or ground was strong and natural, needing nothing more than a bit of polishing in order to be presentable and ready for all to stand upon. As a result of the dream she was able to proceed with the work on her house as well as deepen her own spiritual work.

When a dream is enacted on the stage of a house (read: self) we know for sure that the events we are seeing are all about our selves. When people appear, they typically depict diverse aspects of ourselves — alternatively, such a sequence may reveal hidden nuances of how we feel and behave in relationship to others. Quite often we project the Shadow, that part of us we don't want to be, in the form of another person, thus allowing us to experience and integrate those split-off aspects of ourselves. Our house/self can also be the stage on which archetypes such as the Trickster appear to teach us, or on which unresolved biographical issues play themselves out with vivid drama.

But why pay attention to all this, one might ask? Isn't it just as useful to get a good night's sleep? The answer to this has to do with the mysterious link between house and self: the unconscious is trying to help us, and *if we don't receive and heed messages from the unconscious in dream states, we may have to learn the hard way while awake.* We also risk depriving ourselves and our design project of this special contribution from within.

We have already read the story of the woman who spent thousands remodeling her bathroom, only to realize that what she really needed to do all along was work on her relationship with men. At great cost, her house served as a substitute for conscious self-reflection. Here is another story suggesting the possibilities which arise when we choose to consciously work with our house. In this story a man's wife died of cancer and his two children perished in a car wreck shortly thereafter. Months later he returned from a leave of absence and began to totally remodel his house. First he gutted the entire structure and then rebuilt, completely relocating kitchen, baths, bedrooms, doors and windows. This man was well aware that in remodeling the house he was actually purging and healing himself: he was processing grief, letting go of memories, and making himself whole and ready for a new life. His house, which did in fact need rebuilding, served as a vehicle for his inner work because intention, awareness and self-reflection were all activated. In a sense, he took the same approach to house that we would use in the dream state — responding to the energy of symbol and emotion — and he applied it in the everyday waking state by consciously equating house with self.

In dreams, events are charged with symbolic and emotional content, and in dreamwork we open to the healing which that content can provide. Yet there is an additional payoff which comes if we can succeed in applying this same awareness to waking reality, for in the waking state, too, we are on a stage of symbolic reality, where healing forces, disguised as the personalities of those around us, are ready to guide us. The problem is that we are generally too busy and identified with the ego to recognize the richness of the territory, and thus it is only at random moments of peak experience or flow that we get a glimpse of the underlying dynamics. House as a vehicle for spirit is all about this immediate and vital connection to our environment, and dreams serve to restore that awareness. The special meaning of house in dreams reminds us that the physical dream house is in some way our very self, projected all around us.

There are, in fact, cultures such as that of the Australian Aborigines in which what we call the dream state is considered the primary reality and our waking state is seen as a secondary realm which merely reflects the Dreamtime. Who can say which view is correct? What we can say with certainty is that as our appreciation of the symbolic quality of dreams deepens, we can carry that same awareness into the waking state and better understand the symbolic content of our material abode and the life we live within it. We can relax the need to take any dogmatic approach to dream interpretation. Rather, as house becomes an increasingly living metaphor, we can simply develop a deeper symbolic awareness in which all experience of house, whether waking or dreaming, bears messages from the unconscious, serves as a mirror in our process of self-reflection, and mediates between ourselves and our environment.

Designing Through Dreams

As the distinctions between waking and dreaming begin to blur, it is actually possible to design one's house in dreams — or, to put it more accurately, to see one's house being designed. Here begins a particularly enjoyable interplay between the physical house and the self/dreamhouse.

Beyond cultivating dreaming awareness and forming an intention for dream design, there is absolutely no blueprint for designing through dreams. My own experience has been that dream images of architectural details have presented themselves sporadically over a period of years — sometimes concentrated over several nights, but sometimes occurring just once every few months. There have been many transformational images in particular: hallways, passages, stairways and doors. Other dreams have ranged from complete furnished rooms to minute architectural details such as nichos, lamps, handpainted woodwork and tiles. Swirling patterns of energy have solidified and appeared painted on walls as geometric grids resembling pottery or weaving motifs. The vast majority of images have been of interior details. Pieced together, it is as if a house has been slowly constructed in Dreamtime.

Beyond an occasional sketch such as the mandalas demonstrated in Chapter Twelve, I have avoided imposing architectural drawings on my dream designs. I am wary of "freezing" the process by introducing a left-brain approach — rather, I am content to let the dreamhouse build itself gradually in step with my own growth, trusting that I will know when the time has come to render it in stone. However, the experiences of the Dreamtime have certainly taken my professional work to a new level of "designing from the inside out." Dreams have helped me become much more adept at letting preconceived thought dissolve in favor of allowing image and form to appear on their own.

A wonderful aspect of dream images has to do with the distinctive lowerworld and upperworld energies they bear. For example, very earthy and enclosed interiors convey the energy of the Mother while airy, skylit, and high-ceilinged rooms definitely bespeak the Heavenly Father. These forms often have a powerful mythic or magical quality transcending time and even space. I once dreamed of a round earthen meditation room with a floor which was actually a huge living turtle — the Dreambuilder is not generally concerned with trifling middleworld details! So my job is to fully take in the energy of Turtle (a primal symbol of Mother Earth carrying her home on her back and exhibiting especially wise and fecund qualities) and eventually translate vision to paper, ultimately rendering lower- and upperworld energies in middleworld stone. As it turned out, a beautiful flagstone treatment of the turtle shell came to me weeks later in a breathwork session.

Interior Design

If the terms *dream house* and *remodeling* are not rich enough in double meaning, try *interior design*: one could write an entire book about the parallels between interiors of our houses and the interiors of our psyches. In this context it is doubly noteworthy that dream images of houses are predominantly of *interiors*.

Surely, all of us know what it is to feel peaceful and relaxed in response to certain built environments. There are several aspects to our experience of space, the first few roughly corresponding to our five senses. The visual experience is the most obvious, and the one towards which interior designers strongly lean. Acoustics, by comparison, are seldom appreciated, and in this country no attention whatsoever is given to olfactory experience, even though we have the same physiology as those cultures where sense of smell is highly differentiated. Yet acoustics and smell are very powerful: earth, wood and fabric provide a soothing auditory atmosphere which drywall and tile cannot approximate. Similarly, natural materials and cleaning products emit a pleasing and healthy aroma which is in stark contrast to the synthetics, toxic glues and cleansers found in most homes.

Architecture, more than any art form except dance, relies on *kinesthetic* experience: far from simply seeing with our eyes, we experience the environment viscerally as we move through it. All the senses interact with the physical space in a dynamism which is unique in the arts. Here the totality of our bodies either feels at home or does not. This is primarily a matter of body wisdom, of an awareness which occurs at a level deeper than thought. And so, once again, a successful interior is likely to come from those same deep levels of our being where psyche is close to archetype and instinct. No less than primitive man, we seek at times the protection of a womb-like cave, while at others we prefer the exhilaration of a promontory. Experience of space is strongly conditioned by millennia of living in nature, and in this we, as a species, like both variety and balance.

There are as many dimensions to the experience of interior design as there are to our very complex human being. The connection between homes and the womb is an excellent example, and one which has obvious archetypal overtones. On the face of it, "room as womb" amounts to nothing more than a general human liking of cozy and comfortable spaces. The early psychoanalyst Otto Rank provided a little more precision by observing that the shape of primitive homes demonstrates an instinctive remembrance of the womb. But one could look deeper into the birth process, as has Stanislav Grof in his work with the perinatal matrices, and articulate many nuances of the birth experience which correlate with adult preferences for interiors which are small or large, light or dark, flamboyant or subdued.

It should come as no surprise that the most powerful underpinnings of interior design spring from primal, collective or universal factors. To list a few examples: *symbols of transformation* might express themselves through the interplay of opposites such as light and dark, through an opening from a dim passageway into a bright living room, or through a living relationship to the four directions.

The skillful use of *natural materials* such as stone and timber call to our own nature and to elemental forces, as do *natural forms* such as curves, free-form arches, and recesses. The divine proportion and *sacred geometry* found in pyramids, temples and cathedrals are also potent carriers of energy. But no less powerful are design elements which complement our own instincts and archetypal nature, harking all the way back to our evolutionary past in the cave. Christopher Alexander has attempted to identify many of these in *A Pattern Language* — for example, it seems to be universal that we take comfort in intimate spaces such as alcoves and windowseats, just as we all like to have our backs protected as we take in a big view. As a species we are simply programmed to work in certain ways. Then, too, there are ancestral and cultural components which call us to more particular relationships with hearth and home. Floors will never mean the same thing to a westerner as they do to Asians who for centuries have worked, eaten and communed on the primal ground.

Next to the forces of nature as they exist within and without us, cultural conditioning is actually quite secondary, while considerations of style are weak indeed. The great pity is that in our culture style rules the day, and we have largely forgotten that powerfully transformative design comes from deeper levels. As we noted earlier, the all-important thing is to become transparent to the Creative, knowing that our individual stamp will be made as the creative energy passes through us. Only at the right time do style, conditioning and preferences effectively enter in, along with whatever skillfulness, experience, or professional training we might bring to the drawing board.

All of us have preferences based on biographical experience. We all gravitate to certain styles, be they traditional or contemporary. And each of us has a different background of experience and training, or leanings towards visual or kinesthetic acuity. Our systems of symbol and meaning may be strongly conditioned by culture and family. Add to these the influence of region, microclimate, and budget, and the result is a myriad of factors which guarantee a unique design. But it is the underlying, archetypal nature of the house which, in harmony with our own psychic nature, provides the real energy and raw material for the work. Thus we return full circle to the essential journey of Archetype Design.

Jung's Tower

As we conclude this chapter it seems fitting to refer again to Carl Jung, who in his own journey mapped so much of this terrain for us. In *Memories, Dreams, Reflections* Jung describes the house he built in Switzerland beginning in 1922. His oft-quoted story begins as follows:

> *"Gradually...I was able to put my fantasies and the contents of the unconscious on a solid footing. Words and paper, however, did not seem real enough to me; something more was needed. I had to achieve a kind of representation in stone of my innermost thoughts and of the knowledge I had acquired. Or, to put it another way, I had to make a confession of faith in stone. That was the beginning of the Tower."*

(p. 223)

Jung's description of his intentions for the Tower are, obviously, similar to our own. Yet his journey had a distinct flavor:

> *"From the beginning I felt the Tower as in some way a place of maturation – a maternal womb or a maternal figure in which I could become what I was, what I am and will be. It gave me a feeling as if I were being reborn in stone. It is thus a concretization of the individuation process, a memorial aere perennius. During the building work, of course, I never considered these matters. I built the house in sections, always following the concrete needs of the moment. It might also be said that I built it in a kind of dream. Only afterward did I see how all the parts fitted together and that a meaningful form had resulted: a symbol of psychic wholeness. At Bollingen I am in the midst of my true life, I am most deeply myself."*

{p. 225}

Jung's Tower was built without electricity, central heat, or running water — not because these systems were unavailable, but because he wanted to create a house which pointed "backward to things of long ago."

> *"Our souls as well as our bodies are composed of individual elements which were already present in the ranks of our ancestors. The "newness" in the individual psyche is an endlessly varied recombination of age-old components. Body and soul therefore have an intensely historical character and find no proper place in what is new, in things that have just come into being. That is to say, our ancestral components are only partly at home in such things. We are very far from having finished completely with the Middle Ages, classical antiquity, and primivity, as our modern psyches pretend. Nevertheless, we have plunged down a cataract of progress which sweeps us on into the future with ever wilder violence the farther it takes us from our roots...It is precisely the loss of connection with the past, our uprootedness, which has given rise to the "discontents" of civilization and to such a flurry and haste that we live more in the future and its chimerical promises of a golden age than in the present, with which our whole evolutionary background has not caught up."*

(p. 235)

Reconnecting with our past, taken deeply, is a way of reclaiming and gathering to ourselves the powerful and immense legacy of wisdom which is encoded in the world around us and in our very bodies. At that point it doesn't matter whether we choose a contemporary style or a traditional one, because we are positioned to design a house that can be a living expression of all that we are. Placing ourselves on a continuum with our past, we can build dream houses which serve as capable vehicles on our journey into the future.

COUPLES AND COMMUNITY

Chapter Eight

The open heart soars into supernal realms on transcendent wings of freedom and truth. Transfigured by the spiritual ascent, the two become one. This image is from the Sufi tradition, and resembles the winged solar disc of ancient Egypt. Today, the Harley-Davidson motorcycle logo promises us the same freedom through strikingly similar imagery.

Though most couples hesitate to admit it, a nagging doubt lurks in the minds of many prospective homebuilders: how can we stay married and build our dreamhouse? If homebuilding is such an intensely personal process, how can we possibly make the transition to designing as a twosome?

Couples have good reason to fear for their relationships, for the building business is filled with sad tales of couples breaking up in the course of a house project. People who are supposedly in love wrangle endlessly over every decision and often continue to hold on to resentments years after the house is built. Remodeling and decorating are often just as rugged. In the case of older couples, it is not unheard of for a partner to unexpectedly die soon after a project is completed. Experienced architects have seen these phenomena again and again, but are usually untrained in this area and are utterly unprepared to be of help. Yet this is exactly where help is badly needed, and where even limited effort can bring huge results. In response, Archetype Design treats the design-build process as a unique opportunity for couples to grow as well as to consciously build their future.

By now the reader should understand how emotionally charged housebuilding can be, for in chapter after chapter we have remarked on how deeply house is connected to our self. Actually, we *want* to charge our home with emotion — but we want to be sure it's the right kind by releasing and transforming outmoded and destructive emotions from the very start. Our homes touch and activate every level of our human being, from the most lofty spiritual aspirations to the darkest pockets of hurt, hatred and fear. Relationships tend to amplify all these emotions. It's easy to overlook this truth going into a project — but when the bulldozers begin to roll and the cash starts flying out the door, reality sets in fast. The heat and dust of a construction project present what may be the worst possible conditions for a couple to start working on their relationship.

Left to themselves, most couples will find their own ways of coping — but though the relationship might survive the stress of building, the result may fall far short of house as a vehicle for spirit. Take for example the oldtime arrangement by which the husband is in charge of the money (he holds the power) and the wife gets to be in charge of the kitchen inside his castle. Or the opposite extreme: she runs the show, and his job is to write the checks and reply "Yes, Dear" to her every wish, trying his best to "stay out of the doghouse." Between these time-honored but somewhat twisted strategies lies the deadly middleground of compromise: "I'll take the living room, dining room and kitchen — you take the den, the patio, and the garage, and we can do the bedroom and bath together."

I once helped a couple design a stunning Compromise House. The wife staked out as her territory a magnificent kitchen, an art studio, and a home office. At the far end of the house her husband created an enormous recreation room where he could hole up with his multi-media center and pool table. Between their two domains was an undersized living room which lacked anything resembling an inviting conversation area. The house was well-sited and beautifully detailed — and it was also rather sad. Theirs was a house with two hearts and no center in which to meet.

Home Is Where The Heart Is

By contrast, when two people work to *complement* and support each other, they are likely to build a home in which the distinct parts work together to create a living whole. This is a case of the design reflecting a healthy relationship. In short, design work is effective and easy to the extent that couples have mastered the basics of how to listen, how to express themselves, how to resolve differences, and how to make decisions.

While these four skills happen to be the mainstays of couples counseling, it's clear that therapy is not everyone's cup of tea. Nor is therapy part of the Archetype Design program. However, this leaves us in a dilemma, because it is impossible to do an effective job of journeying into creativity and transformation while sidestepping the very details of lifestyle and emotion over which couples come to grief. Like it or not, we have to be ready to deal with everything that arises on the journey, be it high archetypal drama or gut-wrenching confrontations over the choice of a kitchen sink. In our context the solution is to accept homebuilding as a fresh and unique opportunity to know ourselves and to create ourselves anew. After all, it's a time-limited commitment with a lot at stake and a big pay-off for doing it right. For when we design our house, we also design our relationships.

What might be termed therapy in another context is viewed as skillfulness and creativity in Archetype Design. Chapter Sixteen is entirely devoted to *skillfulness*, systematically addressing issues of communication, problem-solving and stress management as they apply to couples designing together. Such nuts-and-bolts work, though cognitive rather than archetypal, is included for the simple reason that it is so badly needed — the deepest archetypal work still needs to be supported by skillful modes of relating. These are tools and techniques which we learn at the level of the thinking mind, and they lend themselves well to being practiced at home or in the therapist's office. Meanwhile, in this chapter we will continue with the now-familiar themes of creativity and transformation.

It is when we begin to turn up *unconscious* material relating to building that Archetype Design comes into its own, for the metaphor of house as self gives us an amazing tool for harnessing the psychic forces at play and channeling them into creative outcomes. The first unconscious level to emerge is the personal unconscious, which is our individual reserve of forgotten memories, buried wounds, and previous conditioning. As we go to the drawing board, it often becomes apparent that *the physical spaces we seek to create indicate pockets of unresolved emotional material left from childhood experiences of home.* For example, the wish for a dimly lit bedroom might stem from forgotten memories of a six year-old holing up in a comforting "secret place" under grandma's stairs. So far, so good. . . but if one's partner just has to have a really *bright* room with a view because *she* used to curl up in grandma's attic dormer, then it's a set-up for war. What follows can become an eye-popping struggle over the merits of light and dark bedrooms, each partner citing definitive esoteric and architectural precedents and resorting to all manner of inventive and outrageous ploys to secure victory. But all the debate misses the point, for what is really at stake is not bedroom design, but different childhood memories! It almost never fails that blow-ups over design details have little to do with the ostensible bone of contention, but instead stem from unfulfilled or unresolved biographical experiences. The impasse begins to break up as soon as we correctly identify the source of the problem, which in this case are differing associations with comfort and security held over from life at grandma's house.

It's no wonder that both architects and clients avoid opening this pandora's box, because it is all too easy to become mired in a complex web of psycho-emotional forces which defy our attempts at resolution. But in Archetype Design we can refer right back to the essential method for our journeys:

First, we form the intention to journey inside for healing and information.

Second, we enter a non-ordinary state or go to a higher vantage point, temporarily suspending our judging and planning mind.

Third, we fully receive whatever experience or insight comes along, trusting that it has been sent by our inner healer or guide. Rather than push away painful objects and cling to the pleasant ones, we respond by just breathing through them all, penetrating to the center of the experience until resolution and insight occur.

Fourth, we return to ordinary consciousness and the work at hand, bearing creative vision and energy.

Approaching emotional snags in this manner effectively robs them of their potential to hinder us, and in fact converts their energy into transformation and creativity. It is an experiential approach, not an analytical one, and it is one which relieves us of the cumbersome work of having to either analyze or suppress our feelings, freeing us to move ahead without fear. With practice, we can learn to apply this same response to events of everyday reality as they arise, without having to take time out from activity.

Let's see how this template applies to the struggle over light and dark bedrooms. First, the sheer amount of energy which has been stirred up serves as a red flag telling us to back off and investigate. Presumably we have made a contract (an intention) to resolve such issues at their source, and so we proceed to do just that. Sometimes a useful shortcut is to ask ourselves, "How old am I at this moment?" (More often than not, the answer will place us squarely in a childhood context.) Beginning by calming the mind with a meditation technique, we might choose to journey directly into the layers of emotion. Hot anger is probably at the surface, a desperate wanting is very likely below that, and deeper still may be hurt and a nameless but vast fear. The feelings might be clothed in memories of grandma's house or of some childhood insult, and quite possibly they will stimulate other memories and feelings as well. We simply experience them all, breathing deeply and opening the heart — if necessary, weeping or venting as long-held feelings flow out. There's practically no mental effort required, beyond sticking with the experience and allowing healing to occur. And then a miracle just might happen, because if we penetrate deep enough, beneath our darkest fear lies nothing but love. We are *home* again.

If we do this kind of work, and do it well, the focus shifts from winning the struggle to achieving a mutual healing. At this point it doesn't matter *emotionally* what kind of bedroom we build — rather, we can return to our quest and allow deeper, universal energies to shape the bedroom design. House has now been transformed from an emotional battleground to a vehicle of spirit. We will return to this example of bedroom design after looking at how deeper levels of the unconscious can contribute to designing as a couple.

Familial and Cultural Conditioning

As the transpersonal journey continues beyond the realm of the personal unconscious we find deeper and progressively more collective dimensions to our relationships. The first set of these is what Ken Wilber terms the *biosocial*, "the internalized matrix of cultural premises, familial relationships, and social glosses, as well as the all-pervading social institutions of language, logic, ethics, and law." (Walsh & Vaughan, p.24) Here is a set of factors which can either unite a couple or precipitate clashes, and we deal with them in much the same way as in the previous example.

A famously volatile area of difference between partners is *boundaries*. For example, it would be predictable for an only-child to have a completely different sense of boundaries from a partner who grew up in a rowdy family of eight. Whereas only-children tend to have very discreet boundaries and greatly value their personal space, people who grew up with many siblings are likely to have very flexible boundaries; alternatively, if either family-of-origin were dysfunctional there might be no boundaries at all. At the drawing board such differences would typically surface as conflicting ideas about how spaces and rooms should be segmented. But boundary issues can also affect the design process in terms of how decisions are made and who makes the rules. Here again, when the red flag has gone up, we work to penetrate to the roots of conflict and strip it of the emotional content which can potentially explode upon us. In this case it's not necessarily the *boundaries* that matter: both systems may be equally valid. The sore spot lies in the original taboo — the deepseated fear of the child within who knows that something terrible will happen if boundaries are either violated or imposed. Once this fear is penetrated and resolved, the couple is free to renegotiate their decision-making protocol and go on to create a design which accommodates their needs without binding them to the past.

The method of penetrating deeper than the presenting problem inevitably leads to a sharing of common ground, because beneath the layers of familial and cultural conditioning all humans share much the same psyche. To anchor oneself to this common identity can be a potent tool for couples. It is as if one central tree trunk were divided into two great branches: whereas in times of stress there is a tendency to focus on the two opposed branches, our practice is to focus on the single trunk and its roots. When we are in conflict, it is always useful to refer to our oneness and bring it to bear on the situation at hand.

We have already seen how the personal ego-mind becomes stretched and softened when we return from the transpersonal journey. Every such increment of transformation will inevitably contribute to a couple's success as the sense of self expands, the heart opens wider, and personal needs diminish in favor of the collective need. Thus the simple process of journeying, be it in the form of meditation, breathwork, or dance, prepares individuals to function well in relationship.

Anima & Animus

Our experiences of commonality become progressively more powerful as we move past the biosocial levels and into the transpersonal realm. Visiting the archetypal sources of creativity, we also gain access to primordial archetypes of the masculine-feminine which can provide enduring underpinnings for our relationships even as they connect us to the yin/yang dynamic of life itself.

A key archetype for couples is the pair of Anima and Animus, of which we had a glimpse in Chapter Three. In simplified form this Jungian theory says that for an adult, the primary mode of relating to both the inner and the outer world is the relationship to the opposite sex. Anima (the feminine) and Animus (the masculine) together form the archetype of relationship — the basic dynamic of how things work.

A man's inner feminine, or other half, is termed the Anima; a woman's complement is the Animus. These are fundamental, inner structures of the psyche, but in very deep relationships the partner can actually come to personify one's other half. *Complement* is the operative word, reflecting the simple truth that when we reach out to a member of the other sex, we are tacitly acknowledging that she or he has something we need to feel complete. (The same dynamic works in same-sex relationships to the degree that there is an energetic male-female polarity.) So a highly conscious partnership acknowledges the wonderful and mysterious way in which one's partner can "carry" one's own completion.

Rarely, however, are relationships quite so clear. Far more commonly we begin a relationship by projecting our desires and expectations onto a new partner, often failing utterly to see who that partner actually is. Meanwhile, at an archetypal level of which we are usually unaware, we continue to yearn for union with our other half. Thus matters can become considerably confused: overlooking our partner's genuine personality, we take the projected images of our desires and graft them onto the primordial template of Anima or Animus. To make matters even worse, *we may be thoroughly intoxicated from the power of the archetype* which has become clothed in the image of this idealized partner. Usually we call this "falling in love."

However, it's just a matter of time before we begin to see who our partner actually is — which is precisely when many relationships grind to a complete halt. The reason is that, beneath the veneer of projections, the real human being before our eyes embodies at least some of what we must integrate in order to become whole. This is a deeper level of work, and one which many are simply not prepared to undergo. For the relationship to continue, we must be willing to allow the dynamic of Anima/Animus to take us beyond the veils of projection and into a process of seeing the partner and ourselves clearly, all the while becoming more complete as individuals. In real terms this means letting go of our projections and letting life speak to us through our partner, who is nothing less than Anima or Animus personified. When we open to our partner in this way, the power of archetypal dynamics begins to work for us in the interests of wholeness. This, approximately, is the Jungian view, and it is a good one for us because it provides a means of coming into alignment with fundamental patterns and energies which can boost us on our way. Dreams, inner journeys and general archetypal awareness will all come to our assistance. Now, instead of grappling with our partner, we may view him or her as a messenger or bearer of our own completion.

To see how this theory can be applied to homebuilding, let's return to our discussion of bedroom design. We've learned to defuse the unresolved emotional landmines which were blocking progress, but we are still faced with the need to come up with a plan which satisfies both partners without becoming just another compromise. A good place to begin is by recognizing that one's partner is the key — that he or she holds some quality or some secret that we ourselves need in this case. A parallel path is to look to one's *inner* masculine or feminine for the same message — this of course is the bridge to the unconscious, and so we might expect to see additional clues coming symbolically through a dream of one's partner or of another opposite-sex figure. Archetypal encounters of gods and goddesses on inner journeys might also propel one forward at this juncture. This is most definitely intuitive, emotional, right-brain work: it's not so much a matter of figuring anything out as it is of simply opening to one's other half and allowing the energy to perform its magic. It can't be hurried — and when the work is done, we generally know it.

It's not hard to imagine how such an approach might transform what had been a struggle over bedroom design. First of all, one's mate is no longer seen as an antagonist, but is embraced as a divine partner — that alone is a lifechanging step for most of us. Next, the opposing bedroom ideas which had previously been irreconcilable can now be appreciated as complementary expressions of nurturing and expansiveness. Last, both partners have actually expanded their sense of self to embrace a collective vision which encompasses both the security of a womb-like space and the sensuousness of a sunlit view. The result, which might be a soft and feminine sleeping area with a cozy windowseat off to the side, will be an enjoyable and healing space for the two people, both as a couple and as individuals.

The Divine Couple

The archetype of the Divine Couple is one with which we are all familiar. Wedding ceremonies in most traditions allude to the idea of the divine marriage through symbol or scripture. Royalty has certainly represented this archetype over the centuries, and indeed in archaic times the royal couple were explicitly considered to be the embodiment of universal harmony. Our culture tried hard to fit the Kennedys to this archetype, and we tried again with Prince Charles and Princess Diana. And, of course, we reach for the Divine Couple again and again in the leading gentlemen and ladies of the movies.

In former times family structures and reverence for ancestors provided templates for relationships, with the family patriarch and matriarch providing a living example. Mythology has also provided effective representations of the archetype. For example, Krishna and Radha are the passionate divine lovers of Hindu lore, still celebrated in devotional singing which rivals any ecstasy to which our own gospel singers aspire. Shiva and Shakti, embodying the male potential and the vast fecundity of the earth, are invoked both in song and in deep meditation. Tibetan *tankas* typically portray the union of wisdom and compassion as intertwined cosmic lovers with which the practitioner merges in contemplation. We have already explored at length ways of penetrating the symbol of Yin/Yang, which represents the same energies in abstracted form. Quite often these figures appear spontaneously in dreams and breathwork sessions, and in recent decades Westerners in great numbers have benefited from exploring these archetypes and the devotional or contemplative practices which go with them. The archetype of the Divine Couple goes far beyond our conventional notion of role model — Shiva and Shakti, for example, are as profound and dynamic a symbol as can be, and by dissolving our egos and merging with them in contemplation or ecstasy we gain access to the same cosmic attributes latent within ourselves. As Divine Couple, we become the microcosm of the very yin and yang which manifest the entire universe.

In our culture we need the archetype of relationship more than ever, but the available representations — celebrities, royalty, and movie stars — are simply not equal to the task. Nor are the mythological couples, powerful though they are, universally and exactly appropriate for our day and age. In some ways we are left on our own again. Romantic love has saved us from centuries of arranged marriages — but although we all pursue it, romance has hardly proved to be a reliable template for healing and lasting relationships. We can continue to enjoy romance, but we also need to go deeper. The Sacred Journey, in which couples walk hand-in-hand on the path to Wholeness — towards something greater than themselves — may provide a workable context to both carry us into the future and generate a new template for relationship.

From Microcosm to Community

What is true for couples work is largely true for community — after all, a couple is simply a community of two, and the archetype of relationship is certainly vast enough to accommodate more complex human society. This, of course, was well known to ancient sages such as the Taoists and Confucians, who argued that as it went with the family, so it would go with the province and, ultimately, the kingdom. This same sentiment is echoed, albeit in distorted form, in America's preoccupation with lost family values.

If indeed it all starts at home, then we are on the right track as we attempt to make our houses vessels for strong and vibrant relationships. All of the techniques for couples work in this chapter and in Chapter Sixteen can prepare us to successfully live and work with families and groups as well.

It was said earlier that no home has ever made complete sense except in the context of community. The statement is worth repeating, because it bespeaks a truth which has become lost in the rush of urban and suburban sprawl. It used to be that everyone lived in villages and neighborhoods — those have been the primary social and economic systems throughout the formative course of human evolution. Our ancestors depended on community for sheer survival, and our *whole being* evolved in a community context. So, too, our dwellings were either communal, or grouped in circles, or in later times distributed around the vital social centers called villages. Those longhouses, huts, and farmhouses all had a clearcut relationship to each other and to the center, expressing a cosmology or a myth in which every dwelling was part of the larger circle. Until recently even our own cities had distinct neighborhoods with many of the same characteristics.

Only in the last decades have demographic and economic changes erased the place of community on our lives, offering little to replace it. True, we have attained a level of powerful and creative individuality, but at a price. We live in relative isolation, and nuclear families — those that stay together at all — are under tremendous pressure to fulfill needs that have historically been met collectively by relatives, neighbors, friends and elders. Community as we have always known it simply does not exist, and our society is crying out as a result. No school or method of design is worth pursuing if it doesn't address this lack.

Attempting to return to the past is not the solution. Not only are we are far too mobile to fit an old model of community, but the existing infrastructure poses a formidable obstacle to change. As a people we are busy chasing independence and prosperity, while survival no longer depends upon banding together as in the past. Beyond limited social experiments, it is difficult to envision a new model of community on a mass scale. It is far more likely that community, if we are to have it again, will be something entirely new and unforeseeable, emerging from the warp and woof of the moment. Therefore, rather than look outwards for a source of community which does not exist, the answer may be to look *within*. Community is eternally available at the level of archetype and can guide us on towards the outward fulfillment of our needs.

Nevertheless we must not ignore the many important expressions of community spirit all around us, especially in the forms of social service which individuals and organizations offer every day. The urge to feed the hungry, to care for the helpless or to preserve the environment is the very essence of feeling connected to others. The sense of community is also alive in churches and spiritual communities where, as in service, participants share a common purpose or vision which is greater than themselves. The vision of Archetype Design is that this same spirit will be cultivated and reflected in our homes through fundamental simplicity, sustainable building systems, and by increasingly collective planning and sharing of resources.

The new myth of the Sacred Journey is one which recognizes that we cannot travel alone. Although Archetype Design leads us on individual journeys for creativity and transformation, it constantly returns our focus to community through small group sharing, artwork, and ceremony. Central to all these practices is the use of the circle — the timeless, ancestral form of councils, of ceremony, and of telling stories around the fire. To sit in such circles is to array ourselves in a living mandala of community, offering the experience of being one voice in a collective awareness or effort. Cutting through the isolation and fear which is so characteristic of our culture, these practices ride on the interplay between our identities as individuals and as a collective, in effect preparing us to be community members.

All group or community practices – be they meditations, prayer meetings, town hall meetings or drum circles – proceed on the assumption that we can form a collective self which is capable of generating energies and acheivements which surpass what the individual can do. This could take the shape of a new and broader wisdom, more powerful movements of love or reverence, or holistic forms of public works. There may be quite intentional efforts to access a collective unconscious at the level of circle, congregation, or tribe. What has traditionally worked for shamans, healers, and councils of elders can help us now as we explore strategies for living and working as groups and community. Consensus born of collective consciousness certainly is more likely to bring us together than the tired convention of majority rule.

Circle practices are supported and enriched at the individual level by transpersonal experiences. Visions of circles, spirals, mandalas, and other symbols of wholeness are archetypal patterns in our subconscious which leave a powerful imprint – so much so that we begin to see the outer world in terms of these same patterns and themes. The cycles of life and all lifeforms become living reality and a source of great wisdom. To this are added experiences of connectedness with the circle of humanity, the biosphere, and the entire universe. Little by little we become carriers of this vision.

We have much work to do on ourselves, both as individuals and couples, before we will be prepared to live collectively. Anyone who has ever lived in an intentional community knows that dwelling in groups is no easy undertaking. Yet it is equally apparent that a certain spirit arises in congregations, consensus groups and councils which seems to have a life of its own, far greater than the sum of the individuals. This is very hopeful, for such a community spirit has the capacity to guide us and lift us far beyond ourselves to a new collective vision.

THE ARCHETYPES OF NATURE

Chapter Nine

One of Nature's most beautiful forms, the nautilus shell displays the graceful unfolding of the spiral and the sacred geometry of the Golden Proportion.

E xploring the archetypes of nature quickly presents a list of fascinating questions. Why is it that lightning has the same shape as the roots of plants? Why do edible plants tend to have five petals, while poisonous ones have six? Why is the spiral geometry of the nautilus shell governed by the same proportions as the butterfly, the daisy flower, musical harmonies, and bones of extinct dinosaurs, as well as the human body itself? The answers to these questions point directly to archetypal commonality between humans and the natural world.

It should come as no surprise that the forms of nature call deeply to our own inner nature. As a species we have evolved for many thousands of years in intimate contact with the natural world, and the patterns and forms of that world are deeply imprinted on our bodies and on our psyches — thus it is only when the principles of nature are woven into the the fabric of our houses that our ancestral being feels truly at home. Perhaps this is part of what Carl Jung had in mind when he spoke of restoring the connection with our ancient past.

There is no more dramatic example of this than fire, whose power and transformative potential are so vast that mankind has universally been moved to explain and celebrate it in the great myths. Fire makes nearly all of our creative pursuits possible, and only humans seek to control it — yet when fire is out of control, there is nothing more terrifying and destructive. We all share the legacy of a living relationship with fire which goes back to the very beginning of humanity. Fire has fulfilled the most primal and intimate needs of preparing food, staying warm, and fending off predators. It has been at the center of science, manufacture, war, alchemy, councils, storytelling, and of all social life. On the one hand fire is the central element of sacrificial ritual, while on the other it is the defining characteristic of hell. Of all the elements, it commands the greatest respect. In the mythological terms of Chapter Two, fire is charged with the emotion of fear, and hence it has always been held sacred.

The hearth is directly linked to the archetype of fire, with the result that fireplace and stove are among the two most important objects in any house — so much so that *hearth* is virtually synonymous with *home*. Of course we often lose sight of this fact in the fastfood era, but it's a fact not lost on our evolutionary selves. Home is where the hearth is, and when there is no hearth an essential part of us simply doesn't feel at home. Television is our culture's hollow substitute.

When we manipulate fireplace and stove, we have at our disposal the incredible power which comes from the archetype and our ancient relationship with it. This is why nothing makes a living room succeed like sofas and chairs arrayed around a powerful fireplace. In the same way, it's the skillful placement of the cooktop or range which most determines whether the kitchen works, both functionally and energetically. No amount of fancy finishes and architectural razzle-dazzle can compete with the impact of hearth and the elemental power it wields.

What is true for fire and hearth is true for the countless other manifestations of nature which appear in our homes as door, window, passageway, stairway and bed. Developing this enormous potential is as simple as taking any aspect of the natural world to which we feel especially drawn, and then penetrating to the deepest possible level.

Merging With Nature

In America at the millenium it's as if we just discovered nature. National parks are choked with summertime visitors, eco-tours are becoming major venues, and waves of citydwellers journey to the woods each weekend in their sport utility vehicles. This tremendous interest in nature is a welcome development, and is part of a significant change in how we live and care for the ecosystem. Yet from the vantage point of, for example, a Huichol Indian, our way of approaching nature is riddled with contradictions. We visit the backcountry in our heavy-footed way only to return home on Sunday evening and resume the familiar consumerist lifestyle. Unlike the tribesman whose very identity is inseparable from his environment, our relationship with nature remains skin deep.

Yet there's no going back to the primitive consciousness of the nature-based peoples, however appealing such a romantic return may seem. That consciousness evolved over millennia, was grounded in the urgent imperatives of survival, and seems to be fundamentally incompatible with the modern world, which is why ancient cultures tend to rapidly disintegrate when they encounter the outside. What is needed instead is a new awareness which can restore our connection to the natural world and yet survive in the context of technological, consumerist culture. While we may benefit immensely from ancient wisdom, the ultimate answer, it seems, is for us to break new ground — and the principal tool we have at our disposal is non-ordinary states of consciousness. For when the body-ego dissolves in non-ordinary states, the boundaries between ourselves and the environment dissolve as well, freeing us to experience an identification with the natural world which surpasses any previous notion of connectedness we may have had.

Native American vision quest, the Aboriginal walkabout, and the many shamanic traditions of solitude in the wilderness are all methods to penetrate the mysteries of nature through heightened awareness. Journeying into the heart of nature, in fact, is little different from the inner journey, with one important exception: when we explore nature we sometimes have to expose ourselves to real physical danger and discomfort. Although our fears of the wild are usually disproportionate to the actual dangers, if we behave foolishly in the wilderness we'll soon be dead. Wilderness experience adds a nice touch of realism in which vulnerability must be balanced by skillfulness.

Learning to trust the wild is not an overnight process for a culture as estranged from nature as ours. So we might begin in simple ways — by travelling light, by hiking rather than driving, by learning to see in the dark without flashlights, by quieting our minds and sinking into The Receptive. Thus begins a process of relaxing deeper into an attitude of listening to the voices of the trees, the rocks, and the wind. In short, the key to penetrating nature is to withdraw from the array of supports which usually allow us to override our surroundings. With fewer distractions and comforts, with heightened awareness, and perhaps with the added vulnerability of fasting and solitude, we invite an experience totally different from the standard recreational approach.

Canyon and Mountain

Certain forms of nature have an extraordinary capacity to shape our consciousness. Among the primary landforms these include mountain, valley, plain, canyon, desert, forest, cave, ocean, lake, river and sky. All of them could aptly be called archetypes, and each is mirrored in elements of architecture such as tower, skylight, passageway and fountain. Whether we know it or not, in seeking a destination in the natural world we are actually in pursuit of the distinctive mindstates they create: water is soothing, mountains are uplifting, sky is boundless, and caves are mysterious. Knowing these landforms and their energies, we can skillfully use them in the design of our homes.

An excellent pair of examples is *canyon* and *mountain*, which have obvious lower- and upperworld characteristics. These realms are latent in us as well, and therefore when the archetypal energies are rendered in the forms of our house, of course the corresponding energies will be awakened within us. It is a type of pattern recognition: because the pattern exists in our psyche, we can recognize it outside ourselves, and in turn the pattern outside of us can activate the pattern inside.

Canyon is the archetypal journey by which we leave the plateau of human habitation and descend into the recesses of the lowerworld, the realm of mystery. Dropping beneath the canyon rim, suddenly we can no longer see into the distance, and as we descend deeper, the experience becomes an increasingly *interior* one of floor underfoot, walls around us, and the sky ever more remote. The light changes, becoming dimmer and weak. Detail, rather than vista, becomes dominant: the shapes of outcroppings and ledges, the patina of the centuries, the textures and patterns of the vegetation. Perspective and spatial relationships appear distorted by the verticality of the experience and by the shifting of backdrop as we move through the canyon's sinuous turns. Life forms seem to be amplified by the quietude of this enclosed world: animal presences are strong and palpable, and cries of swallow and owl echo starkly off the sandstone. At the canyon floor where water may be found, diverse species exist in profusion along the watery ribbons of life. Here, with the light so far above, the feeling is profoundly feminine. It is a watery, riverine, almost uterine environment where the juices of Mother Earth wind endlessly on their return to the sea. Even the rocks, sculpted by the millennia, bear the marks of water in their color and shape. The passageways twisting through the rock are the birth canal, arches and corridors are the yoni of the earth. The deeper one goes, the more intense the experience becomes, and at times one feels almost claustrophobic — consciousness is somehow compressed and driven within. Even the animal life is predominantly reptilian. Moods become dark and primal, dreams are murky, and (especially if one is fasting and meditating) the psychic reality is a parallel one of descent through layers of depression, sadness, and fear. Only after one has completed the psychic descent does the experience open into one of insight and a sense of being held in the recesses of Mother Earth.

Mountain, by contrast, is the ascent toward the heaven realms, the realm of the gods, a journey to the upperworld. It is an experience of mastery — certainly in the sense of transcending the gross everyday world, but also in the sense of self-mastery and attaining higher truth. Leaving the teeming plains and valleys, we climb to higher and less frequented regions. Excitement mounts despite the arduous climb, and the very act of deep breathing puts us in an elevated state of mind. Everything becomes more rarified — the forest, the animals, the air itself — as we climb higher. Awareness, too, becomes expansive and vast. Here, where we are exposed to sun and sky, the elements of fire and air are dominant and we enjoy a commanding view of the horizon and all that is below. Peaks and overlooks resemble towers and turrets of defense, and the shapes are pre-eminently craggy, phallic, masculine. The climb itself features elements of willfulness, conquest, domination. Yet it is here, right at the edge of survival, that we traditionally find the abodes of hermits and monks who make their retreat high above the business of humanity. Reaching the peak, we touch the sky, the realm of higher truth, of light, and of the gods. And though we can see the whole world below us, in fact it is transcendent inspiration which is the essential mountain experience, and one which we can take home with us. Touching the realm of the gods, we also touch the Self within. But the experience at the summit is necessarily brief, for no man or woman can linger long at these heights.

Penetrating the mysteries of canyon and mountain is an easy way of helping us infuse our homes with tangible lower- and upperworld qualities. *Canyon* would typically find its expression in rooms with dimmer light and a distinctly interior feel, such as dens, meditation rooms, bedrooms and hallways. The water element might show up specifically in bathrooms, greenhouses, or atriums. Arches, doors and passageways especially can carry the canyonlike quality of birth and transformation. The same themes can be rendered in details such as stone floors, sculpted curves, ledges and niches, small skylights, fireplaces, fountains, and downward spiralling stairs. Finishes such as soft plaster and stone can accentuate the lowerworld feeling, as can soft lighting and the right choice of color and texture.

By contrast, the attributes of mountain are best rendered in spaces which are very light and airy. Of course, upstairs rooms come immediately to mind, such as lofts, studios, roof decks, towers, and all rooms with big views and lots of windows. Skylights and clerestory windows allow light and sky to flood in from above, while large windows afford commanding views. Upward spiralling stairs, landings and mezzanines all convey the mountain experience. Details such as high ceilings and wood beams are appropriate here, as are stone fireplaces. Wood and stone are the dominant mountain elements, while the upperworld quality can be further developed with light finishes, soft fabrics, and furnishings and artwork which are uplifting or celestial in nature.

Interestingly, what might be an upperworld experience in the light of day can shift dramatically when the sun goes down and windows and skylights fade into the background. Nighttime lighting will determine whether a bright room retains its vibrant upperworld quality or shifts in a more restful and interior direction. While a well-lit room may serve well for parties and festive moments, a more cozy and subdued setting around the fireplace is generally what the body seeks at the end of the day. In fact, our energetic needs change throughout the daylong cycle of the sun, being more active and energized during the day and increasingly quiescent and receptive into the evening. So it is that when the sun goes down our ancestral self still seeks the comfort and protection of cave and hearth.

Between mountain and canyon lies the busy middleworld of valley and plain. Kitchens, bathrooms, home offices, entryways and utility rooms will tend to be dominated by more functional aspects, yet they too may reflect aspects of canyon and mountain. The end result may be a house which offers a dynamic balance between masculine and feminine, light and dark, rest and activity, sky and earth.

While our example has been the theme of canyon and mountain, some individuals might be more attracted to the contrasts of land and sea, or perhaps to the archetypes of river, desert, or forest. Which landform we prefer is not important, for all the archetypes of nature lie within us, and each can reconnect us to both the earth and to our selves.

The Structures of Nature

Nature reveals an entirely different level of primary or archetypal forms when we shift our focus to the very small or the very large. Under the microscope, objects are made up of spirals, circles, triangles, pentagons, hexagons, pagodas, and pyramids. Curves and arcs are governed by characteristic proportions, and forms are arrayed, layered, rotated, and repeated by similar mathematics and geometry. The very same shapes and proportions occur at the macroscopic level, from the vortex of tropical storms to the dazzling spiral of our own galaxy. Sacred geometry, far from being a purely intellectual accomplishment, has a solid basis in the concrete world, displaying in ziggurat, pyramid, acropolis and cathedral the timeless and universal proportions of nature.

Perhaps the most ubiquitous of such shapes is the spiral. We see it in seashells, the curling of smoke, and the whirling of hurricane and tornado. Spirals are frequently *paired* as in the double helix of DNA, or are *dinergic* (opposed) as in the center of flowers or the kaleidoscope of peacock feathers. Leaves twirl to earth, spiders spin their webs, and snakes coil — all in spirals. Significantly, the geometry of spiral forms such as the nautilus shell displays the same Golden Proportion which informs much of great classical architecture. More simply, the structural attributes of the spiral have long shown up in traditional construction techniques: in how tipi poles are stacked, in the compression roofs of Navaho hogans, in basketry or the rope method of pottery.

Other archetypal forms, though less evident to the naked eye, are equally pervasive. For example, energy and particles move in waves and often have wavelike patterns of growth. Crystalline structures exist all around us, appearing in substances as humble as salt or as celebrated as diamonds. This is the complex geometry of hexagons and polyhedrons, combined with the mystery of those forces which bind elements together to produce the most durable and precious of forms.

The Forces and Processes of Nature

Looking deeper than the material forms of nature, we can observe numerous patterns and flows of energy which underlie physical reality *and are also evident in our own bodies and psyches*. Some of these chief themes are as follows:

1. *The visible cycle of death-and-rebirth.* Most clearly seen in the sequence of plant and seed, the cycle of the four seasons, and the rhythm of day-and-night, death-and-rebirth is the most basic cycle of existence and the most common theme in the great myths as well as in much of our own literature. The very word "nature" means "that which is born." In our psyches, this cycle is played out as the sequence of ego-death and spiritual rebirth, which is the fundamental dynamic of spiritual growth. The quadrated circle, the wheel, and the ouroboros are symbols closely related to death-and-rebirth.

Transformation — changing from one form to another — is virtually synonymous with death-and-rebirth and manifests as a relatively short list of basic patterns. The list includes fractals — the pattern which, for example, causes a shoreline to display the same contours whether we view it microscopically or from a satellite view. It includes repetition, as in the scales of a fish, the reproduction of an insect, or the thousands of leaves on a tree. The spiral is one such pattern, as is the concentricity seen in ripples spreading out over a pond. Entropy is a well-known example. Gnomonic expansion is the process by which forms simultaneously repeat and expand. And perhaps most interesting — and for many of us quite new — is the phenomenon of the Mandelbrot set, a mathematical formula which allows a set of variables to endlessly develop, change, disintegrate and re-emerge anew. When displayed on a computer screen, the Mandelbrot set has an amazing resemblance to yantras, mandalas, and to the vortex frequently encountered on the inner journey in holotropic breathwork and shamanic visions. Consciousness itself mirrors nature, evolving in a *spiral* fashion, *repeating* familiar themes but at a higher level; like *fractals* our concepts and images proliferate, and through *entropy* we achieve momentary stasis. Yet whatever shape or pattern transformation takes, change ultimately occurs through a leap from the known to the unknown.

2. *The chaos and violence of volcano, wind, wildfire, earthquake, and lightning.* Modern man prefers to forget how overwhelming the forces of nature can be, but in truth an appreciation of nature's power is a traditional check against pride and ego. Destruction is an integral part of the death-rebirth cycle, and it is found within us as well as in nature. We have volcanic eruptions of anger, experience earthshaking truths, are blown away by sudden revelations, are consumed by desire, and have lightning-like flashes of inspiration which instantly rearrange our thinking. Chaos, in other words, is the counterpart to the ordering principles of nature and is a force to be recognized and embraced.

3. *The blessings of sun and rain.* All indigenous peoples know that life proceeds from sun and rain, and their cultural and spiritual lives are substantially focused on maintaining the harmony with nature which will ensure such continued blessings. At a pragmatic level, primitive man knew quite well how to pick solar sites for cliff dwellings and how to settle near perennial water sources. Mythologically, the gods of sun and rain have always been prominent. Symbolically, we experience sun and rain as the light of awareness and the waters of life.

4. *The cycles of sun, moon and stars.* Again, traditional cultures developed sophisticated relationships with the cosmic forces affecting the seasons, agriculture, healing, and spiritual undertakings. For this reason astronomy and mathematics were the first sciences, permitting mankind to place himself in alignment with the planets and seasons. Ziggurats, pyramids and megaliths were sited according to astronomical observations, while the lore of the planets and constellations described the archetypal aspect of the celestial beings. Sacred buildings usually faced the rising sun of the east and were frequently aligned precisely with the dawning rays of summer solstice. Worldwide, astrology continues to be a powerful way of relating our psyches to these archetypal forces of the cosmos.

5. *The medicine power of plants and animals.* All ancient cultures, having long been in close contact with nature, know intimately the attributes of plants and animals. Physically, each species has its particular value when taken as food or medicine. Certain plants have special psychoactive properties and have been regarded as sacred food of the gods. Similarly, animals have distinct personalities or energies which affect us to the degree we are receptive to them. For shamans, animals appear both physically and in visions as spirit messengers, allies and teachers. Physiologically, we know that our own neocortex is just the most recent evolutionary layer grafted upon a mammalian brain and a primitive reptilian brainstem. Indeed, our animal nature runs deeper than most of us would like to think.

6. *The play of the opposites.* Night and day, life and death, male and female, sun and moon are the most familiar of the many polarities which comprise life. The symbol of Yin and Yang is perhaps the most profound expression of this truth, and the sixty-four hexagons of the *I Ching* are a description of the infinite differentiation which occurs when yin and yang interrelate. Careful attention to the play of opposites in house design can produce a structure of many dimensions and wonderful variety in which both the eye and the spirit have many places to go.

States of Consciousness and Interconnectedness

Clearly, the world of nature presents a tableau of unimaginable complexity which far surpasses the ability of our intellect to understand. Some would call this *mystery*—and indeed, it is only through extraordinary modes of perception that we are presently able to grasp the totality of any phenomenon.

Science may provide a thorough and useful description of material characteristics, but only in non-ordinary or holotropic states of consciousness are we are able to experience the deepest level of interconnectedness with plants, animals, and landforms. Going deeper still, the patterns and energies by which nature moves are frequently revealed to be the same as the patterns within us. Indeed, when the boundaries separating us from the world completely fall away, we may have the unitive experiences known as *satori, nirvana,* or enlightenment, momentarily merging with individual lifeforms, the biosphere or even the entire cosmos. Anyone who has had such an experience knows how utterly transformational this can be. For example, when we have experienced plants and animals as "all our relations," it becomes extremely difficult to think of using pesticides and herbicides, or to live in any way which could compromise ecosystems or destroy habitat.

The ability to experience nature at an archetypal level is directly analogous to Jung's description of allowing the archetypes to arise "from the forgotten depths" rather than merely perceiving them intellectually. Such archetypal encounters offer transformative potential which far surpasses ordinary recreational pursuits, placing the essence of sacred geometry and sustainable architecture within our grasp. Exploring the complementarity of our inner/outer nature, sacred geometry becomes a matter of direct perception rather than academic study (even though we may still choose to undertake such studies). Sensing the flow of energy between us and our environment, *feng shui* becomes an intuitive reality rather than a formal system from a faraway land. And merging with the forces of season, sun, and earth allows sustainable ways of living and building to become "second nature" rather than optional techniques which we overlay on other design priorities.

Sadly, most people are not drawn to sustainability simply because they have never experienced interconnectedness with the natural world. Material comfort and security are all they know, and they tend to reject a sustainable lifestyle because they associate it with having to give up familiar and comfortable modes of living. The key, in other words, is to shift to a new ethic and a new worldview in which the relationship to nature, both within and without, becomes joyful and rewarding enough to displace the creature comforts and addictions of old. Such a shift must inevitably be grounded in actual experience rather than in intellectual study alone.

Clearly, the awareness which results from a deep investigation of the forces of nature is altogether different from the mainstream consciousness of our culture. It is an awareness which offers us a pathway to our own nature and enables us to develop homes in harmony with both the environment and our own inner being. Of all the possible paths proposed in Archetype Design, the nature path is the most accessible, posing little theoretical challenge while being available to all.

SPIRIT AND SUSTAINABILITY

Chapter Ten

The sacred circle is twice-quadrated through the unfolding of a flower, symbolizing the sustaining nature of death-and-rebirth through the lifecycle of plant, blossom, and seed. At the center is the bindu dot, representing the separate consciousness which flowers into an awareness of its own wholeness.

Our appreciation of nature and its archetypes, however genuine and heartfelt it may be, is terribly at odds with the effect our civilization is actually having on the earth. Developments such as global warming and the vanishing ozone layer are daily serving notice that our current lifestyle cannot continue and must be radically changed. Yet, by an incredible feat of denial, we continue to overlook the fact that we are on a collision course with the earth's capacity to support a growing population and an expanding consumer economy.

To call the dominant issue of our time an environmental crisis is to miss the point entirely, for in truth the crisis is a human one. The question is not whether the earth will continue to exist, but whether mankind can survive manmade degradation of the planet. The deteriorating environment is a direct reflection of our own dis-ease, and the healing of the ecosystem can only proceed from our own healing — or from our well-earned demise. In effect we are in a deep moral dilemma which can only be resolved by understanding thoroughly the dimensions of the problem and then, as in all moral dilemmas, by performing the painstaking spiritual work of relinquishing selfish and destructive habits in favor of those which promote the common good. Moreover, all indications are that, for the forseeable future, the spiritual path and the path of sustainability are identical.

The Dimensions of Sustainability

Sustainability is the buzzword which lies at the heart of the environmental debate. Simply put, sustainability requires that we develop new ways of living within the limits of what the earth can support. Conserving resources, eliminating pollution, and maintaining ecosystems are the mainstays of the program — but although these concepts appear straightforward, the task of implementation is so enormous as to be mind-numbing. We are just beginning to comprehend that, with our very survival at stake, the quest for sustainability is likely to be the goal of every human endeavor for at least the next century. The problem is extremely serious and the outcome very much in doubt — yet the one hopeful note is that this quest, more than any in history, has the potential of being a unifying force for global society as well as a catalyst for a new vision of human destiny.

Whereas sustainability is as yet a vague term for many of us, it is actually rather simple. Something is sustainable if it can be supported or upheld over time. By itself, sustainability is a neutral term which can refer to any type of system, whether it is benign or destructive. Thus economists seek sustainable growth (which tends to degrade the environment) while ecologists specify sustainable levels of resource utilization (ostensibly to preserve it). So it is the context which really gives meaning to the word sustainability. Our context, of course, is the effort to maintain a human presence on the planet.

The all-important criteria for sustainability lies in the relationship between systems, because a system (in this case, the human family) can only be said to be sustainable if it may be supported without depleting other essential systems (such as the ecosystem). But there are thousands of sub-systems in the human realm which affect even greater numbers of sub-systems in the biosphere, so it's easy to see that the workings of sustainability are far more complex than we generally realize. The situation is so complex, in fact, that most of us recoil from the problem, preferring to bury our heads in the sand and await the arrival of a technological fix. Such a response, however, amounts to out-and-out denial, depriving us of any proactive agenda at the same time that it exacerbates the crisis.

It is said that the Buddha acknowledged just one miracle: that while all around us people are seen to grow old and die, each of us wants to think that it will never happen to us. Our situation viz-a-vis the biosphere is much the same, for despite twenty years of increasing global temperatures even the well-informed among us tend to remain indifferent to the problem or dismiss global warming as a short-term cycle which will correct itself. We'd really like to think that ozone depletion can be remedied by sunscreen. Similarly, although world population is increasing by 60 million a year, the mind just doesn't want to believe that global demand will inevitably outstrip the availability of fuel, food and water.

The indicators of environmental distress are indeed alarming, and it doesn't require genius to conclude that it will require an enormous effort to adjust to such developments, let alone solve them. Even the most dazzling technological breakthrough, though it may patch the ozone layer, provide clean energy, or feed the planet, will not necessarily restore ecological balance or generate a satisfying quality of life for billions of people. While technology seeks to make its contribution from the top down, our equally important task is to implement a viable lifestyle from the bottom up — at the most basic level of food, shelter, and clothing. This, of course, is where our work as designers and homeowners comes in, for here we have a direct effect on the environment in the way we build and heat homes, power appliances, irrigate the landscape, and dispose of waste.

A Sustainable Lifestyle

At this very moment all of us have ready access to affordable technologies which can make a significant reduction in our environmental impact at the cost of very minimal changes in lifestyle. For example, energy can be saved in even the grayest climates of the northwest and northeast by simply orienting houses to face the wintertime sun, placing plenty of windows on the south, and insulating thoroughly. A solar pre-heater can provide the initial 40% of water heating while an on-demand water heater can finish the job without having to keep forty gallons of water hot around the clock. In this way it is child's play to reduce fuel consumption by at least 25%, and the accompanying change in habits amounts to nothing more than running the shower at reduced pressure, setting the thermostat a few degrees cooler, or turning off electric lights when leaving a room.

The same approach applies to the other systems which comprise a house, such as water. Flow-reducing fittings automatically conserve water at sinks and showers, which we can augment by shutting the water off altogether while we brush our teeth. Hardy native plants can replace the showy perennials and lush lawns which suck up both water and chemicals. We can direct roofwater to trees and shrubs which need extra moisture, while in rural areas we can pipe wastewater to orchards and gardens. With little effort, huge quantities of water can be saved, with the added benefit of enhancing our relationship to the immediate ecosystem.

Another oft-overlooked area is the use of native and non-toxic building materials. Any native material such as stone or timber will spare us from the toxic out-gassing associated with processed materials as well as require less energy to transport and manufacture. Other natural materials such as wood or stone floors (instead of synthetic carpets) or tile countertops (replacing plastic laminates) can drastically reduce exposure to harmful chemicals as well as unhook us from the petrochemical industry. In addition to being non-toxic, certain "alternative" wall systems such as straw bale, light clay, pumice-crete or rastra block are notably energy-efficient, use recycled or renewable materials, and create a wonderfully solid and organic living space. Few people who have had the experience of living in a home made of such natural materials would ever consider reverting to a synthetic environment.

These are just a few alternatives which reduce environmental impact, save money, preserve health, and actually shift our source of satisfaction away from consumerism and towards a meaningful interaction with the community, the local economy, and the immediate environment. So the obvious question is this: if a sustainable lifestyle is so available and offers so many advantages, why aren't we all living this way?

Why Sustainable Building Has Not Caught On

There are important lessons to be drawn from moments in recent history when Americans briefly flirted with sustainability. The first was the oil crisis of 1974, which was a shocking wake-up call for a people whose main interest had been in creating the world's first consumer culture. Designers and engineers threw themselves into a dramatic effort to conserve energy, and the results included the birth of what we now call sustainable building. Exhorted by President Carter to tackle the problem "with the moral equivalent of war," Americans complied by turning down thermostats, carpooling, and installing insulating batts in the attic. But as the oil flowed once again and a new administration removed economic incentives, most people simply regressed to their former patterns of consumption. There was a brief revival of environmental interest following Earth Day 1992, this time featuring efforts to recycle, plant trees, and introduce environmental programs in the schools. However, while environmental awareness and activism has most certainly increased, for the most part our lifestyle has stayed the same. Alternative building systems and products, however effective, have remained a marginal phenomenon. Even in the Southwest, where sunlight is abundant and free, relatively few homes take advantage of solar energy.

The core problem is that, given a choice between comfort and a lifestyle which requires a little more restraint, people tend to choose comfort every time. Certainly this is characteristic of our culture, and probably of human nature as well. The lesson seems to be that changes in behavior which are imposed by external crises typically do not endure once the conditions of crisis are resolved. Rather, what has to be changed are the underlying *causes* of the crisis — in this case, our selfish and short-sighted attraction to creature comforts and, by extension, to the whole web of wealth and power which supports them.

A second lesson is that, like it or not, culture changes even more slowly than do individuals. So while a crisis might stimulate a flurry of sudden change, it takes time to consolidate substantial shifts in attitudes and lifestyles. Despite the sense of urgency which many of us feel, we must acknowledge that the transition to sustainability is likely to be a longterm proposition.

The status of solar heating is a perfect case in point. The technology of letting wintertime sunlight penetrate a building through south-facing windows is about as simple as can be — Anasazi cliff-dwellers knew all about it a thousand years ago. Today's solar enthusiasts have successfully built houses which are *entirely* heated and powered by the sun, yet very few homebuyers gravitate to these structures, primarily because too many needs for beauty or comfort are overlooked. Mainstream homeowners dislike those long, unbroken stretches of glass which look like some sort of solar factory. Moreover, the interiors of such buildings often lack the amenities and gracefulness which most people crave in a home. Both aesthetically and functionally, solar homes pose too radical a shift.

These very same householders, however, are generally quite open to designs which incorporate limited sustainability features, as long as they retain enough amenities and attractive design elements to make them feel at ease. Most people sincerely want to live in harmony with the environment, just as they want to feel more connected to others and be more happy. This, in fact, is the majority of homeowners — and so here is an enormous potential, for if an entire generation of new homes and remodels were even *ten percent* solar-heated, the cumulative savings in energy and fossil fuel emissions would be vastly greater than that of a relatively few totally solar houses. Even more significant, the culture as a whole would have made an initial step towards sustainability which will enable the next generation to leapfrog even further. The same goes for the long list which includes roofwater collection, recycling, gray water systems, permacultural landuse, public transportation and community living.

Sustainable home designers will simply not achieve large-scale objectives if their work is so cutting-edge that it leaves the marketplace behind. Thus, our task as designers is to take pioneering innovations and implement them slowly, in pace with cultural change. Meanwhile the American people, who are nothing if not pragmatic, need to embark on a hands-on experiment in sustainable living which is incremental, enjoyable, and well-supported by collective participation.

The Path of Sustainability

The simple fact is that a sustainable lifestyle is reducible to a relatively small number of systems or components, each of which offers a workable point of entry to this new way of living. Actually we have all been making a start at recycling and conserving resources during the last two decades — we just haven't been very successful at taking isolated acts of earthwise living and weaving them into a new ethic or a collective worldview. So to regard sustainability as a path in itself — and to do so in a concerted way — is actually a powerful departure from past efforts.

Let's take water conservation as an example. As a consequence of state and federal legislation, almost all plumbing fixtures now have water reducing features which cut flow rates by about half. All of us are therefore using less water than we did ten years ago, though it's not necessarily a deliberate act. But if take the next step of shutting off the water while we load the dishwasher, we've made a conscious commitment to water conservation. . . and if we also shorten our morning shower by a couple of minutes and reduce the frequency of toilet flushes, then — presto! we've made a significant change. If, in addition, we take the time to inform ourselves about potable water sources (reservoirs, aquifers, deep wells, water treatment plants) and the various methods of wastewater treatment (septic systems, sewage treatment plants, effluents poured into rivers and oceans), then we begin to get a panoramic view of water issues. At one end of the picture we might understand our connection to the politics of dammed rivers and blocked salmon runs, while closer to home we can see how phosphate-laden detergents find their way to groundwater, eventually destroying freshwater habitat. Now we are in a position to weigh our individual responsibility in problems which had previously seemed far beyond our ability to either understand or to influence.

The same process works for any of the systems we employ at home. Recycling links us in a tangible way to both the preservation of resources and the greater cycle of death-and-rebirth. Solar heating and electricity can most obviously reduce fossil-fuel emissions, but they also redefine our relationship to the oil industry and to the politics of the Persian Gulf. Similarly, the use of non-toxic products and organic food reduces pollution of both the environment and our bodies — but it will also challenge the established healthcare system and subtly shape marketplace forces in favor of the emerging holistic worldview.

Exploring sustainable living in this way bestows several benefits. First and most important, every action, however small, is a commitment to "walk our talk" and bring our lives into alignment with what we know to be true. Each commitment also makes the next action possible. Engaging and informing ourselves lets us understand the consequences of our actions, empowering us to act with kindness and wisdom. No longer mere theory, sustainability becomes an experiential method of engaging with the processes of nature. As the web of interconnectedness begins to reveal itself, we can navigate the pathways between habitat, other species and the human realm while doing harm to none. We see how economic systems, political systems and ecosystems interface, and we can learn to work skillfully within them. Indeed, the concept of wholeness is confirmed, not merely at a theoretical level, but pragmatically through the details of daily life.

The Spiritual Underpinnings of Sustainability

As we enter the 21st century, the evolution of human consciousness appears to be so much in convergence with planetary needs that we can virtually equate spirituality with sustainability. Theoretically, the expansion of self towards wholeness must inevitably break through the shell of selfishness to encompass all of humanity, all other species, and the ecosystem of which we all are members. This vision of wholeness points unambiguously towards practical results in the form of a sustainable lifestyle which does no harm to others. And just as clearly, sustainability claims its spiritual roots in a worldview in which all men are brothers and all creatures are our relations.

The transpersonal journeys and techniques explored in the earlier chapters all have as their goal the development of just such a holistic worldview, without which we lack both the guidance and the inspiration to heal ourselves and our ways of living. But while this visionary and transformational work is indispensable, a different set of tools is needed if we are to translate our ideals into action. These are the tools of discipline and self-sacrifice, which are the traditional work horses of spiritual practice.

However, a cautionary word about spirituality may be useful at this juncture. We have noted, in the history of myth, how the notion of the sacred originally referred to those realms which lay beyond man's understanding and control. We went on to see how the secular has gradually edged out the sacred, to the point where modern man behaves as if he is the master of his universe. Now, however, the environmental crisis is exposing the fallacy of this illusion and we are awakening to a much greater picture in which we are asked to serve as stewards, not masters, of the world around us. We are once again learning to live in harmony with the environment, but unlike the shamans of old, we are doing so in a distinctly secular way. One could say that the sacred is re-emerging as the secular, rendering conventional concepts of spirituality rather less relevant, and announcing a new era in which the values of non-harming and compassion are less the achievements of spiritual adepts and more the hallmark of ordinary human behavior. In a time when the gap between vision and practice absolutely must be narrowed, any spirituality which focuses on non-material concerns to the exclusion of physical reality may actually hinder efforts to ground our ideals in effective, concrete action.

Nevertheless there is no getting around the fact that foregoing personal desires in favor of the common good is plain, hard work which relies upon the same discipline and surrender long associated with spiritual practice. Such qualities do not come easy to Americans. While other nations have been forced to band together and make do with little, we have been busy indulging in the luxury of the American Dream. Yet the ideals of self-sacrifice and collective effort are deeply embedded in both our spiritual and political traditions and are ready to be taken up at any time. As a people we have repeatedly demonstrated the ability to join together in times of adversity. The very big difference is that while the enemy may formerly have been Nazism or communism, today the enemies are the forces of greed, fear and ignorance which dwell inside all of us.

In the present context, a simple and demonstrable teaching may be all we need — and that teaching is in fact available in the popular aphorisms which we all know but take for granted. The Golden Rule, for example, tells us everything we have to know about how to conduct ourselves. "Slow and steady goes far in a day" is very much to the point, while "never bite the hand which feeds you" is right on the mark when it comes to redefining our place in the ecosystem. So, while we might enjoy the so-called higher teachings, they are not actually necessary. Folk wisdom is perfectly adequate for those who prefer a more worldly path.

It is impossible to reflect on these themes without remembering Mahatma Gandhi, whose gift for distilling the deepest spiritual truths into prescriptions for practical action transformed an entire nation from powerlessness and servitude to dignity and self-determination. Few of his teachings were any more complicated than the Golden Rule or the notion of walking one's talk, yet his slogan of *satyagraha* — often translated as soul-force — took the colorless idea of discipline and transformed it through a vision of moral authority and selflessness into a non-violent force for good such as the world as rarely seen.

The problems facing us are not so different from those India faced fifty years ago: the present impoverishment of the biosphere can aptly be compared to the grinding poverty of Gandhi's countrymen, while India's subservience to the British very much resembles our own inner struggle with ignorance, fear and greed. Today, no less than in Gandhi's time, the global predicament requires an inspiration and a powerful resolve which are equal to the challenge itself. If we find our motivation flagging, we will do well to remember these words:

> *"The golden rule...is resolutely to refuse to have what millions cannot. This ability to refuse will not descend upon us all of a sudden. The first thing is to cultivate the mental attitude that will not have possessions or facilities denied to millions, and the next immediate thing is to rearrange our lives as fast as possible in accordance with that mentality...whenever you are in doubt or when the self (ego) becomes too much with you, try the following expedient: Recall the face of the poorest and most helpless man you have ever seen and ask yourself if the step you contemplate is going to be of any use to him."*
>
> — Mohandas Gandhi, *Young India*, 24 June 1926

Sustainability and the Archetype of Wholeness

Although sustainability is a relatively new concept — we've thought about it for only a few decades — it can certainly claim a strong foundation in the archetype of wholeness, within which sustainability operates as a particularly dynamic attribute. As we know by now, contemplating or merging with archetypal symbols is a primary method of becoming transparent to creative and healing energy, and so to investigate the various symbols of wholeness is appropriate at this point. We could start by looking at the circle — but while the circle conveys a great deal about universality and fullness, it says very little about the relatedness or dynamism inherent to sustainability. Somehow we need to chunk the field of limitless potential down to bitesized pathways and guidelines which we can actually use.

If we were to create a dynamic symbol of sustainability, the next graphic step might be to add a dot in the center of the circle. In the tantric tradition this dot is called the bindu, and it represents the individual consciousness. Now we have the two protagonists — the individual and the totality — and with them the possibility of a relationship. The bindu needs a way of expanding to become one with the whole, but at the same time the circle individualizes itself as the bindu in what amounts to a two-way road. This pathway manifests archetypally as quaternity, and thus we discover a dynamic which looks like this:

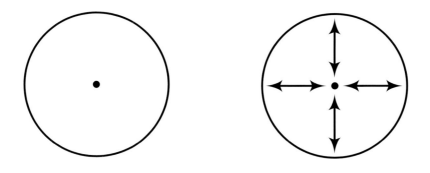

Now, to render the dynamic as one might actually see it during an inner journey, we can replace the arrows with petals of the flower, implying a natural unfolding of the self. The human identity is here subsumed in the idea of life process itself, represented as a plant. We could go on to visualize the center of the petals as a yoni, emphasizing the element of rebirth. The image might look like this:

Our archetype of sustainability is manifesting symbolically as a quadrated circle which encodes information about the nature of time and space itself.
To begin with we have before us the four directions, which is the primary division of space. Mythologically, this is related to the east-west journey of the sun, with the south representing the zenith and the north the nadir of the sun's nighttime underworld journey. The very close practical correlation in terms of solar design is that of rising/setting sun, solar gain from the south, and the cold side of a house on the north. Equally represented in the mandala is the division of time into the four seasons, implying the annual cycle of death-and-rebirth, which is in fact the very matrix within which sustainable modes of living must operate. And of course, the four petals form a cross, symbolizing the human body with arms outstretched as well as the solar myth and the cycle of life-and-death. Last, each opposing pair of petals displays the play of yin-yang opposites which spins the web of the universe.

Understood and visualized in this way, wholeness is no longer an abstraction or a mystical state which can be attained in isolation from "the ten thousand things" which comprise the world. It encompasses the entire universe, and thus the journey (quadration) is one of developing sustaining compassion for all life forms we encounter. The symbol is telling us that the entire pagaent of life occurs as the bindu unfolds to realize wholeness, and that the laws of the universe, both physical and meta-physical, are the pathways we must follow. The magnitude of this play of consciousness is denoted when the petals are doubled to eight or quadrated again to sixteen.

Both the image and its implied concept take an enormous leap when we extrude it to three dimensions. The circle becomes a sphere, providing an image in which identification with the biosphere itself is graphically accurate. Within the sphere, each life form is linked by the web of connectedness:

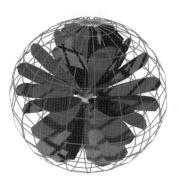

This three-dimensional image not only takes us to the edge of what the human brain can visualize, but it stretches our concepts of space and time as well. The two-dimensional Cartesian grid has been blown into an enormously complex starburst of expanding consciousness, in which everything is happening simultaneously and at many levels of reality, not unlike the Big Bang itself. Images like this are commonly experienced in altered states of consciousness, and not surprisingly are accompanied by transcendent feelings of connectedness and oneness with the infinitely vast universe.

Holographic imagery adds the most recent technological touch to our symbol of sustainability by using laser beams and mirrors to project life-like three-dimensional images into space. (Most of us had our first holographic experience in the opening sequence of Star Wars, when the image of Princess Leia was projected from R2D2). If a holographic image is captured on a photographic plate, it is found that any portion of the image, however small, contains the information needed to generate the entire image all over again. In this way holograms appropriately render the notion that not only is every single life form connected to all others, but each actually encompasses all the rest at another level of reality. Wholeness, in short, is already within us, and the journey is simply one of coming to that realization.

With the concept of sustainability we acknowledge that the task of global healing and balance goes hand in hand with the realization of our own wholeness. And so we are ready to begin the work of mastery — not the former mastery of nature or mastery of the world, but rather the masterful application of the principles of wholeness.

PART TWO

MASTERY

Humbly constructed at the foot of the sacred mountain which it emulates, Taos Pueblo is a masterful example of built myth. Rooftop observances acknowledge the upperworld, while ceremonies deep in the kivas preserve the link to the Mother. Both dimensions inform the ceremonies and village life which take place on the middleworld of the plaza.

MANDALA AS METHOD

Chapter Eleven

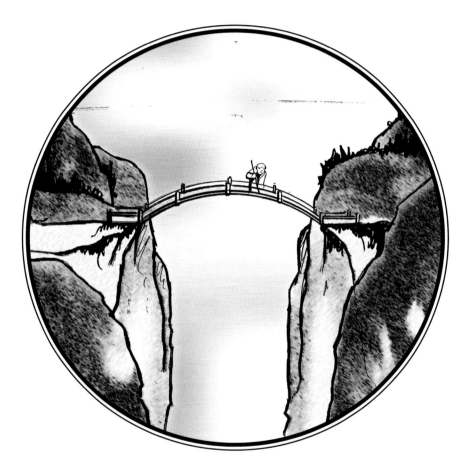

The bridge traditionally symbolizes the link between the conscious mind and the unconscious or superconscious realms. At other times, the bridge is the means of safe passage over turbulent water or deep abysses. In Archetype Design, it is the Mandala which provides the bridge between Mystery and Mastery.

In mythology, after the Hero has ventured into the underworld in quest of the prize, he is faced with a different set of trials on the journey home. Just so in Archetype Design: having penetrated the archetypal sources of creativity, we still need a way of translating creative vision into the forms of architecture. Somehow we must bridge the gap between mystery and mastery, between right-brain and left-brain, without losing the creative essence in the mounting pile of blueprints, bricks and two-by-fours.

Mandala is the method which provides this bridge. We have already encountered mandalas in Chapter Three, and each chapter of this book has begun with some form of mandala. Carl Jung used them therapeutically as a way for his clients to further psychic integration, and Stan Grof has adopted them as a means of bridging the experiences of non-ordinary states and ordinary reality. Fundamentally, mandalas are pictures which record inner experiences in the language of image-and-emotion.

Here we will use mandalas in a rather particular way. First, we want to record our inner vision in a non-linear form — one which preserves as much of the original emotion and energy as possible, and which for the moment completely disregards all practical considerations. This, the first step in the mandala process, concerns purely the mystery, and at this stage it may appear that the mandalas have nothing to do with design. (We know they do of course, because as we design the house, we design the self).

The second step is to slightly shift the focus to design elements or themes. A mandala can express the integrated energy of the house, or its relationship to the cosmos and the immediate environment, or the dynamic between the individuals who will live in the structure. However, we are still working with themes or energy flow, rather than the with design criteria which will come later.

Finally, the focus can narrow to literal displays of site use, sustainability features, or to actual architectural details. Ideally these mandalas will still be highly symbolic or fanciful, allowing the first expressions of architectural form to be loose and imaginative containers for the energy which informs them. With these last mandalas we come right to the edge of the conventional design process.

The mandalas are pregnant with creative vision and energy and are poised to give birth to architectural forms and details as we begin the interface with site conditions, function, materials, and budget.

To illustrate the method, let's look at a series of experiences and mandalas which have produced the design for an addition to my own design studio. I began with the basic idea of creating a circular sacred space where up to a dozen people could gather for meditation, holotropic breathwork, and similar practices. To display the idea as a mandala was straightforward, because the room itself is a virtual mandala. The initial image, showing eight meditators, looked like this:

Eight meditator mandala

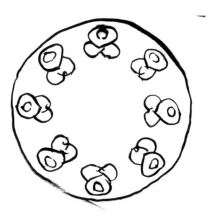

From this initial sketch the vision for the room unfolded in a series of experiences over a six-month period. The first image came midway through a breathwork session when, in a sequence of unrelated visuals, I suddenly saw the blank white wall in the interior of my studio. Next a rippling effect became visible in the wall, and slowly an opening appeared, becoming larger and larger until it stabilized as an unmistakable yoni roughly the size of a passageway for an adult. I knew instantly that this was the entrance to the sacred space, and that the passageway was to be a threshold of rebirth from one consciousness to another. Here is the image drawn in mandala form, accompanied by the eventual construction detail:

Yoni mandala   *Passageway rendering*

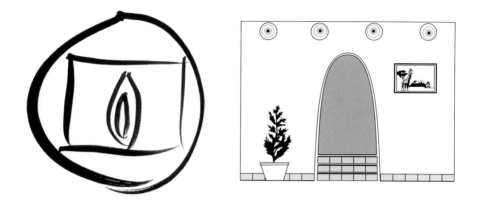

The next development came in a dream in which I was sitting, as in meditation, on the back of a huge living turtle which was the actual floor of the room. From that time on I called it the Turtle Room, and I enjoyed several subsequent visualizations of the floor coming alive with the energy of Turtle. In a later breathwork session I saw how the pattern of the turtle shell could be literally rendered in flagstone. The mandala turned out like this:

Sitting on the turtle

From the very beginning of the project I knew that I wanted to construct a mandala-like ceiling of timbers and saplings which would culminate in a pyramid skylight in the center. However, I had the sense that I was missing something, and a shamanic journey provided the opportunity to look for the remaining piece of the puzzle. In the session I went to my place of power and called Turtle to take me to the Upperworld and show me the secret to the skylight dynamic. Turtle indeed arrived and led me into the sky where we slipped into a fold in the clouds and entered another realm. There I saw the detail, shimmering in the night sky like a constellation of stars with connecting rays of energy patterns. The figure was a pyramid superimposed over a circular structure in such a way that the four points of the base of the pyramid corresponded exactly to the four cardinal points of the base of the circular structure. It was perfect and simple, and the attributes of the geometry continued to unfold through a series of mandalas and drawings.

The Upperworld Journey

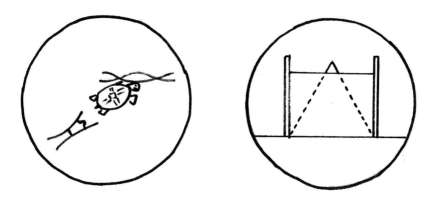

The final vision for the room came in breathwork, in which a line of dancers entered the room in a sacred manner, spiraling clockwise into the center of the room. At times the energy abstracted into a black-and-white geometric grid, not unlike those seen on the pottery of the pueblo tribes. The room was actually modulating in step with the music which was being played for the breathwork session, giving a thrilling insight into the old concept of "architecture as frozen music." So I drew a mandala to record the experience, interpreting the spiral dance first as guidance about moving properly in the room and taking the geometric grid as a pattern which might be painted along the base of the walls.

Spiral dance mandala and sacred grid

The last steps in developing the design consisted of thematic mandalas illustrating the relationship to the four directional cosmos and to the elements themselves — adding another level to the dynamics of the previous mandalas, and developing the sustainability of the previous design.

Four directions / window, fireplace, water, entrance

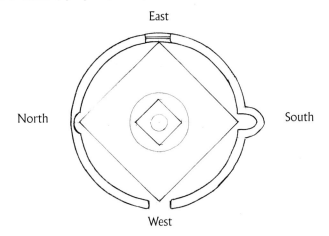

East

North   South

West

With these mandalas the important conceptual design work was complete and all important elements well-anchored in graphic form. It was then possible to slide seamlessly into floor plans, elevations, and section drawings. The same method may be applied to the selection and development of building site, as we will see in the next chapter.

THE SITE

Chapter Twelve

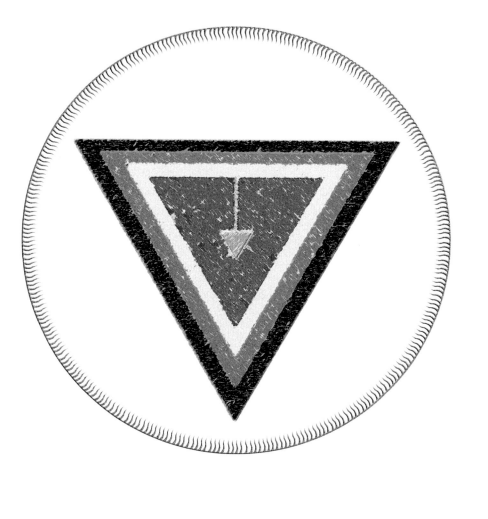

The Kali Yantra encodes the attributes of the Great Mother, primal Shakti, giving birth to all and devouring all.

In almost every case, owner-builders seek out their architect or begin the design process only after they have purchased their building site. This is understandable, for more than anything else, buying land is the commitment which gets the entire project rolling. The problem is that building sites are usually chosen before much thought has been given to design — sites are chosen on account of views, or because of emotional responses which are so powerful as to edge out other design criteria. Frequently the only advisor is the realtor, whose interest of course is in making the sale. All seems well until the clients request a solar house design, only to discover that they've bought a site which does not face the sun! The obvious lesson is that site selection must be done with a comprehensive set of criteria in hand.

Choosing the building site (or buying a house with remodeling prospects) is the first and most important test of whether we are being guided by a new vision of spirit and sustainability. Whereas the American Dream employs criteria dealing primarily with goods and services, the Sacred Journey proposes a new set of conditions which are supraordinate to the traditional ones. So while a proposed site might score high on the ordinary checklist of services, utilities and site conditions, for our purposes it also has to support the higher values of spirit and sustainability. For example, though it is quite desirable to have natural gas for backup heat systems, it is far more important to have good solar exposure so that we can eliminate the need for backup heat right from the start.

Figure 1 summarizes the conventional criteria for site selection and then adds two tiers of higher considerations. We have, in short, a hierarchy of values with Conventional Criteria as a basis, Sustainability Features in the middle, and Spirit of Place at the top.

Figure One:
Spirit of Place
- four directions
- community
- three worlds
- spirit

Sustainability Features

Energy Factors
- solar exposure
- cold air mass
- transportation
- alternative sources

Natural Conditions
- soil conditions
- wind exposure
- water supply
- wildlife habitat
- native plants
- growing season

Manmade Conditions
- sound pollution
- light pollution
- future development
- collective resources

Conventional Criteria

Views and Values
- views
- neighbors
- trees
- property values
- security
- taxes
- codes & covenants

Services and Utilities
- gas, water, sewer, electricity
- roads, transportation
- police, fire, medical
- schools
- shopping, recreation

Physical Conditions
- access
- slope
- drainage

The Conventional Criteria are self-explanatory and quite apparent to most people who are shopping for land or a house. Any good realtor should be prepared to provide detailed information along these lines, so we won't dwell on them here, except to reaffirm the importance of considering every single one.

The next level of *Sustainability Features*, though not difficult to comprehend, may require some professional assistance to perform an actual evaluation. In the list of *Energy Factors*, for example, it's the homeowner who must evaluate how much energy will be consumed in commuting to school or work, weighing that consumption against the advantages of what might be a pristine but remote homestead. But when it comes to solar exposure or alternative energy sources, a consultation with a designer or experienced builder might be useful. Following this procedure is essential: solar design is just not possible on a site where sunlight does not fall, while successful gardening on even the richest bottomland may be significantly compromised by nighttime movements of cold air. While few sites are perfect in every respect, the best decision can only come from being aware of all the forces at play.

Natural Conditions greatly predetermine the possibilities for developing a homesite. Good native groundcover or a robust ecosystem are indicators of favorable topsoil and natural water supply, providing a headstart for landscaping or gardening. Strong winds, on the other hand, generally pose a challenge to almost any activity. Bare earth and erosion suggest that topsoil has been lost and the ecosystem has been disturbed, probably requiring some effort to rebuild topsoil and recontour the land. Polluted surface- or groundwater can pose additional problems for waterwells or food production. On the positive side, wildlife habitat and the presence of animals suggest that all is well with the land. High ground with plenty of sunlight usually indicates less frost and a longer growing season. More subtle are the possibilities of utilizing a gentle slope to support the flow of water, sewage, waste, compost, and supplies.

Manmade conditions are typically negative and for the most part are fairly obvious. Traffic, commercial operations, ugly houses, air pollution and subdivisions are among them. Additionally, any prospective lot or home purchase should also be visited at night to inspect artificial light and sound levels. Daytime inspections will never reveal the downside of distant highway noise or the potential for headlight beams to penetrate your bedroom window at night.

At the peak of our hierarchy we come to *Spirit of Place*, which is in fact a traditional topic in architecture. Architects always want to invoke the spirit of place, but they don't always have the tools to do so. We, however, can summarize spirit of place in terms of the symbolism we have been exploring, and we also have a good array of methods to penetrate the mystery beneath our feet. First we have the horizontal dimension symbolized by the four directions: it encompasses the seasons, the cycles of growth, the natural world, and also the human milieu of community. This is complemented in the vertical dimension by the shamanic cosmology of lower- , middle- , and upperworld that points to the unseen realms of archetype, ancestry and, of course, spirit. We know by now that these themes are better experienced than merely understood, so let's move on to an experiential analysis, pretending that a tract of land has already been purchased and that we are ready to identify the building site.

Finding a Place of Power

The conventional way of developing a building site is to immediately pinpoint the house location (usually on the strength of an emotional or intuitive response). Next comes a review of access and utility requirements, and finally a more technical investigation of gradients, soil conditions, drainage, codes, and so on. Generally the homeowners are all too happy to jumpstart the work by providing an instant site selection. Whether it's eagerness or anxiety, we seem to be in a big rush to fantasize sitting on the sofa taking in the view — but unfortunately, by the time the truly appropriate moment comes to start designing, these early fantasies have often become fixed ideas which block the creative process.

Archetype Design brings different skills and a different protocol to the process of site selection, applying everything we have learned about meditation and non-ordinary states to cultivating a sensitivity to place. Once again it is a progression from mystery to mastery: first we want to unlock the secrets of the land, and then move through a sequence by which the progressively more practical layers of site development are added.

Whether yours is a ten acre estate or a quarter-acre lot, there is a spot on the land which for *you* holds a special attraction or power. This place of power may not be the location for your house — in fact, right now we're deliberately tabling all thoughts of homesite. We are seeking the one spot where your body feels most comfortable, your mind most clear, and your heart most at ease. All we have to do is to find it, and we can do so through an altered state. Finding the place of power is not a mental exercise — you simply won't find it by evaluation and analysis, because the energy you want to sense transmits at a deeper level of awareness. This is where the work with right-brain shift, body awareness, and dissolving the ego-mind pays off.

There are two strategies for walking the land in search of a power spot. You can proceed systematically, perhaps spiraling from the perimeter to the center, or you can randomly roam about. Either will work, but both begin with a centering practice. A good one would be the upper/lowerworld meditation from Chapter Six which grounds us in the body and places us in the ancient relationship to sky above and earth below. This is a big, panoramic awareness which relaxes any narrow goal-oriented focus. Try to maintain this expansive and unfocused state as you move about the land. If you find yourself lingering pleasantly on a particular spot, mark it lightly with ribbon or a pile of rocks and move on. You may find several such spots, but probably you will be drawn back to only two or three candidates.

Once the choices are narrowed down in this way, it is time to focus on specifics. Take a half-hour or more to explore how you feel in each spot, until one place stands out as yours. Above all, see if the body is relaxed and if you feel at ease. Through meditation or inner journey, pay attention to whatever experience arises: images, associations, messages, physical sensations, movements of energy or of light, states of mind. Although the visual experience might be pleasing, take care that the views alone do not determine your selection. This is the means of finding your power spot, as well as of connecting to the land and finding everything it has to tell you.

The land can welcome you, it can heal you, or call out to be healed. Sometimes it will repel you and tell you not to make this your home. But if you are welcomed, then make this spot your *temenos* (sacred place) and begin right away to forge a deeper alliance with the spirit of the land. With ceremony, mark a large circle on the ground with pebbles. Place larger stones accurately at the four cardinal points. If you are so inclined, invoke the powers of the four directions and of the upper and lower directions; call the spirits of all the creatures who live on this land and of all ancestral spirits who have walked it before; ask their protection and guidance as you begin to make this your home, and in return offer your protection of the land. Or, if such ceremony holds no appeal, simply meditate to still the body-mind and bring yourself into harmony with the energies which are present.

This relationship to the land is the basis on which all subsequent intuitions and observations may be layered. As on vision quest, animals may appear which bear significance for you. Plants may reveal their natures, and on inner journey one may even contact the archetypal spirits of these beings. At an elemental level, awareness of the patterns and moods of the wind and of rainfall will increase.

One will come to appreciate the quality of the light at different times of day or season, and one will know the embrace of the night and the rhythms of the moon. In time these impressions will translate into designs for solar gain, natural lighting, and ventilation — but at the beginning, it is enough to know the land, because this knowledge is the mother of all that follows. A mandala is the ideal medium for recording these impressions, as in Figure 2.

Figure 2

It takes discipline to limit the attention to these aspects of the site and to postpone the planning process, but it is worth it. As a culture we have been estranged from the earth and its mysteries for far too long, and it takes considerable tuning to even begin to regain contact with the land. How far one wants to take this part of the work is a matter of choice — but only when you feel solidly grounded in the natural conditions should you extend your attention to the next layer of site characteristics. At about this point it becomes appropriate to select the actual house site so that we can begin collecting specific data. It is also time to rely increasingly on the thinking mind as we proceed to note and evaluate solar potential, soil conditions, slope, drainage, erosion, and the natural plant cover. This is a more dynamic view of how the land actually works — what natural forces and conditions are operating — and it will enable us to work in harmony with those forces and preserve the land. We can observe how the existing drainage, for example, can be used or modified to benefit the plants while not eroding the soil. We might notice that certain plants prefer particular soil and solar exposure.

The angle of the slope might be one which favors heat from the sun in winter, but be overly exposed to afternoon glare in the summer. All these details are better learned onsite than in books. They can be divided into Energy Factors and Natural Conditions and displayed in simple schematics as in Figures 3 and 4.

Figure 3
Energy Factors

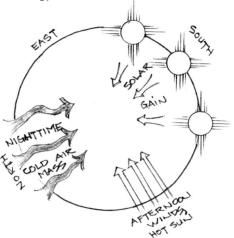

Figure 4
Natural Conditions

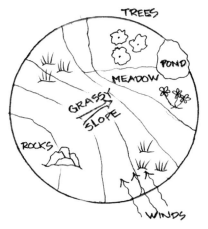

But what if the building site is a small suburban lot, totally devoid of plants and wildlife? Then your job is to bring life back to the land, and the best way to do that is to find a nearby natural site whose characteristics your lot might once have exhibited, and learn everything you can from that place.

The next layer of information deals with man-made surroundings and results in a schematic showing everything which must be screened out, eliminated, or rectified. These include noise pollution, nighttime light pollution, neighboring houses in view, traffic, utilities, and roadway access. Figure 5 shows how to diagram them.

Last, we generate a diagram of our desires for developing the site (Figure 6), primarily showing view corridors and specific outdoor areas. Note that we haven't shown a house yet — we're still working to get all our variables in place. Now, and especially if our diagrams have been made on tracing paper, we can overlay our levels of information and begin to draw some conclusions. We can see immediately where the view corridors are, and how view windows might capture solar gain from the south while avoiding glare from the west. We can imagine where windows can take advantage of prevailing winds for cross-ventilation, or where existing or imported trees can provide cooling shade. We can note where roofwater will have to be treated carefully to prevent erosion. In fact, we have amassed a wealth of information and understanding which puts us in an excellent position to design a house which fits the land, works with natural forces, and makes the best of surrounding man-made conditions. A simple site plan, as seen in Figure 7, is the final Mandala.

Figure 5
Manmade Condiitons

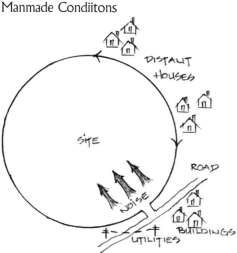

Figure 6
Site Development Goals

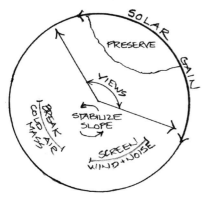

At some point the shift to a formal site plan is made. At a minimum this means starting with a standard survey of the tract, but for sites with steep slopes a topographical survey is extremely useful. Surveyors can also locate the exact location of natural features such as large trees, rock outcroppings or ponds.

Figure 7
Site Plan

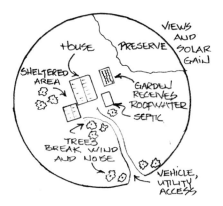

If you have staked out the house site, they can show that on the plan as well. You can now begin to transfer the data from your previous diagrams onto tracings or photocopies of the survey. The goal is to be able to communicate to an architect all the site advantages and problems, together with proposed solutions — or to be ready to work with these conditions yourself.

Surveys will generally show details such as setbacks, utilities, and easements, but they won't show data such as restrictive covenants, architectural guidelines, or development codes which may significantly affect your planning. This research must be done at this juncture, and thus certain restrictions may be added to your survey mark-ups.

With the site plan we begin to run up against technical and legal details which may exceed the ability of novice homebuilders to handle. Now is the time to bring in an architect or designer and form a team — but all the work up to this point is essential for *you* to have done. It's you who must be in harmony with the land you are calling home, and unless you are lucky enough to find an extremely intuitive designer who knows the principles of Archetype Design, you will have to communicate to him or her a vision of land use which few architects share. Your mandalas, diagrams and mark-ups are the tools for making this extremely important communication. But first, you must also develop the "wish list."

THE WISH LIST

Chapter Thirteen

The most famous mandala of tantrism is a complex and mesmerizing play of threes. The downward-pointing triangle, like the pubic delta, represents the feminine shakti, while the upward-pointing triangle is the masculine lingam. Here they repeatedly overlap to form six-pointed stars of wholeness, which immediately dissolve into the next dynamic series.

The author's dining room features a mandala-like table at the center. The roof beams radiate out to the exterior walls, where a series of windows link the occupants to the community and the environment through the energy of the circle.

Having evolved for millennia in settings such as caves and cliff dwellings, it should come as no surprise if humans feel an archetypal sense of comfort and safety in intimate and cozy spaces such as this windowseat.

This great room (above) offers an expansive upperworld experience of sky, sunlight, and sweeping vistas. In the same house, a windowless belowground sitting area (below) offers a contrasting lowerworld atmosphere of intimacy and softness.

This mandala-like ceiling with pyramid skylight is similar to the design described in Chapter Eleven, creating a dynamic flow of energy in the meditation room on the following page.

Passageways, doors, and stairs are actual transitions from one realm of consciousness to another. This stairway creates an aura of mystery and an irresistible urge to ascend to the next level.

A sacred space is an essential part of house as a vehicle for spirit. Sacred space can be as simple as a nicho (above), or as elaborate as the kiva-like meditation room shown below.

The wish list is a straightforward inventory of everything which must be accomodated in the house design, from the type of kitchen sink to the relationship of living room to dining room. At the physical level a house consists of thousands of details, while at the level of energy flow there are numerous key relationships to consider. What follows is a questionaire which I use with my design clients. It is quite comprehensive and ensures that not many details will be left out — but equally important, it raises many questions and stimulates deeper thinking about design parameters.

The questionaire may be supplemented by narrative descriptions, poetry, tear sheets from magazines, photos from coffee table books, or absolutely anything which represents images or feelings related to house design. Just one word of caution, which is to be wary of the mind's tendency to lock prematurely onto literal solutions to the exclusion of the creative vision. The wish list is essential, but it should not edge out the inner work which precedes it.

RESIDENTIAL DESIGN QUESTIONAIRE

This questionaire is intended as much to clarify your goals as it is to give the designer the information needed to prepare a proposal and begin work. It's quite comprehensive — not every question will apply to you, and you might even get a few laughs out if it. But it's a good way to get started. The questionaire is in three parts:

I.   General Data
II. Design Details
III. Sustainability Features

Please answer as best you can...ask questions if you'd like...make notes in the margins or flip sides...and add anything you'd like in the way of reprints, cut sheets, wish lists or narratives.

I. GENERAL DATA

Name(s): _____

Mailing address: _____

Home tel. _____ Work tel. _____

Fax _____

E-mail: _____

Best time and place to call: _____

Size of residence (outside dimensions): _____ square feet.

Size of garage: _____ cars. Extra space for storage or work? __y__n

Additional buildings: guesthouse __y__n size: _____ s.f.

No. of bedrooms _____

Studio __y__n size _____ s.f.

other: _____

_____

_____

Budget for all improvements (not counting design fee): $ _____

Projected date of construction: _____

Desired date of completion: _____

Will you be seeking construction financing? __y__n

Will the house be __owner-built or __contractor-built?

Any considerations such as phased construction or planned
future additions? __n __y

If so, describe: _____

_____

_____

Names and ages of full-time residents: _____

_____

_____

Owners' names and project name as they will appear on the drawings:
(eg. "John and Linda Holmes Residence, Santa Fe, New Mexico")

_____

_____

_____

Street address of new residence:_____

_____

_____

Environmental goals:
__slightly sustainable __moderately __extremely sustainable
Health goals: __avoid the worst toxic materials __as non-toxic as possible

II. DESIGN DETAILS

1. Exterior

Preferred style:_____
- ____ traditional regional style
- ____ contemporary
- ____ traditional with solar/sustainable features
- ____ contemporary with solar/sustainable features
- ____ emphasis on solar and sustainability features
- ____ one-of-a-kind (describe):_____

Exterior walls:

____ 10" adobe	__ 14" adobe	__ 24" adobe
____ 15" poured pumice	__ 18" pumice	__ 24" pumice
____ 2x6 frame/stucco	__ 2x8	__ 2x10
____ 10" rastra block	__ 12" rastra	
____ 18" straw bale	__ 24" straw bale	
____ 12" cob/light clay	__ 18" light clay	
____ other:_____		

_____
- ____ use different materials as appropriate
- ____ not important — leave it to the designer

General notes on finishes:
- ____ rockbottom budget finishes
- ____ rustic & earthy
- ____ standard finishes (varying by region)
- ____ more upscale finishes and craftsmanship
- ____ introduce original or exotic details
- ____ clean & contemporary

2. Room-by-Room Checklist
Check all requested rooms:

___entry

___mudroom

___greenhouse or atrium

___living room

___dining room

___kitchen

___utility (laundry etc)

___pantry   combine with utility? __y __n

___powder room

___den / family / TV & media room

___study / office / library

___art studio

___meditation

___recreation room (billiards, ping pong, play, TV, etc.)

___gym

___master bedroom (detailed questions to follow)

___master bath

___master dressing room / closets

___BR2 __king __queen __twins fireplace: __y__n walk-in clos. __y__n

___BA2 __tub / shower combo __stall shower__bathtub __2 lavs__1 lav

___BR3 __king __queen __twins __fireplace: _y__n

___BA3 __tub / shower combo __stall shower __tub __2 lavs __1 lav

___BA 2 will serve both bedrooms 2 & 3

___storeroom   items to be stored:_____

other: _____

_____

_____

Please specify a "typical" ceiling height (a common scheme is 8' standard throughout and 10' - 12' in the great room):
__feet typical throughout __feet for LR / DR

What rooms, if any, will be upstairs:_____

_____

_____

3. Specs for Principal Rooms
A. Kitchen (list brand names if you have a definite preference)
island __y __n chief function: _____(eg. cooktop, eating, prep)

conventional slide-in range with oven __y__n __gas or __electric?

cooktop: __burners __gas or __electric? __range hood or __downdraft?

wall ovens: standard oven above and below double __y __n

_____ convection above, standard below __y __n

_____ single oven only __standard __convection

_____ ovens __elect. or __gas?

_____ microwave where?_____

refrigerator: side by side __y__n

_____water/ice in refrig door? __y__n

_____refrig drawers in cabinet system __y__n

compactor: __y__n

dishwasher: __y__n __left or __right of sink?

sink: dbl. tub __y__n

_____ stainless or __porcelain?

_____ rim mount or__ undermount?

_____ disposer __y__n

_____ instant hot water __y__n

_____ soap dispenser __y__n

_____ reverse osmosis __y__n

2nd prep sink: __y__n

_____ stainless or __porcelain?

_____ rim mount or__ undermount?

_____ disposer __y__n

_____ soap dispenser __y__n

_____ reverse osmosis __y__n

countertops: __tile __Corian __granite __maple other

for eating/congregating (choose one):

_____ stools behind an island

_____ stools behind a peninsula

_____ breakfast nook with table for 2-4

_____ country kitchen table for four and up

_____ nothing in kitchen

mini desk area in kitchen __y__n

TV in kitchen __y__n

B. LR/DR/Kitchen

Do you prefer formal/traditional separation between these rooms, or an open floor plan which provides functional and aesthetic divisions but creates a "great room" feel? Check:

_____ all three rooms separate
_____ LR and DR open to each other
_____ Kitchen and DR open to each other
_____ all three open to each other

Is the living room likely to be used primarily for entertaining and family events, while the den/family room is where you will spend most of your evenings? __y __n

How many people should the LR seat? _____
Can we avoid having a TV in the LR? __y__n
Do you have a lot of artwork requiring wall space? __y __n
Bookshelves in the living room? __y__n

B. Master Suite

size of bed: _____fireplace in BR __y__n
TV __y __n
Other furniture:_____
2 lavatories __y__n
separate tub and shower __y__n   jets in tub __y__n
larger shower with second shower head __y __n
steam unit for shower__y__n   bench in shower__y__n   bidet __y__n
other amenities:_____
closet preferences:
__walk-in closet: __off bedroom __off bath __between
__an open dressing room arrangement with the closets and dressers arrayed around it.
safe __y__n where?_____
prefer __dressers or __built-ins? locate in __closet __dressing room __ BR

4. Miscellaneous Features

Computerized home management system (controls security, telephone, audio/visual, heating/cooling, fire detection, irrigation, hot tub, and lighting from touchpads or any touchtone phone worldwide) __y__n

Central vacuum system: __y__n

Radiant floor heat: __y __n __ Preferred alternative:_____

Air conditioning __y__n evaporative cooling__y__n

Heat Recovery Ventilation ("HRV" — good for chemical sensitivities and
   allergies) __y__n

Water softener__y__n

Security system __y __n

Distributed audio __y __n video __y __n home theater__y__n

Drip irrigation __y__n

Do you enjoy gardening and landscaping? __y__n

Which landscape approach do you prefer:

__ native plants with low water requirements and maintenance

__ non-natives requiring more water and maintenance

__ non-natives and ornamentals in courtyard areas only

Number of months a year you will be in residence: _____

Probable months of most frequent residence: _____

Probable months of least frequent residence: _____

Will you have a house sitter when away? __y__n __don't know

Any handicapped considerations present/future:

Any environmental sensitivities or special health considerations?

Other amenities:

__porches	__swimming pool	outdoors?__y__n
__courtyard(s)	__lap pool	outdoors?__y__n
__flower gardens	__hot tub	outdoors? __y__n
__vegetable gardens	__fountain(s)	
__orchard	__tennis court	
__dog run	__volleyball court	
__stable	__basketball hoop	
__lawn	__kids' play area	
__other	__sauna	

5. Site Development

Potable water: __ community __ private well __ roofwater
Irrigation: __ same source __ gray water
Gas: __ natural (at property line now?__y__n) __ propane
Electricity: __ public utility (at property line now? __y__n) __photovoltaic
Sewer: __ community system __private septic system
Telephone: how many numbers will you need: __
TV: __ none __ cable __ satellite __ conventional antenna

Road/driveway: any unusual challenges? _____
_____
_____

Parking: number of spaces outside garage: _____
_____

6. Misc. Details

Furniture: please take photographs. On the back of each photo, indicate where the piece should go and what is the width/length/height. This goes for area rugs as well.

Piano? Billiards table? Collections? Any special activities anticipated: music, bridge, painting, mechanics, sewing, meditations, study groups, etc.?

Art objects and paintings: photos with dimensions and probable locations.

Anything else which comes to mind as you do your homework
(feel free to sketch, write wish lists, provide tear sheets from magazines —
whatever it takes to get your ideas across!)

III. Sustainability Features (continued in the next chapter)

SUSTAINABILITY FEATURES

Chapter Fourteen

Across many traditions, Turtle is the maternal symbol of fertility, perseverance and wisdom. She is frequently pictured as supporting the universe on her back, which is encoded here as the cosmogram of the quadrated circle. It is said that the entire I Ching was apprehended spontaneously by meditating on the pattern of a turtle's shell.

S ustainability features comprise the last section of the questionaire which began in the previous chapter – but the details constituting sustainable building systems are so specific and so new to most homeowners as to warrant supportive description. What follows is a continuation of the questionaire with thumbnail sketches of the various building systems which are available.

It is worth remarking on an aspect of systems theory which is extremely relevant to sustainable building systems. Systems do not exist in isolation: they require some kind of input, and they generally produce some kind of output. In building it is just the same: we might seek a benefit such as energy conservation, but we must also consider input, which might be initial investment, maintenance, lifestyle adjustments, or old-fashioned elbow grease.

Newcomers to alternative building always want to know the financial implications of investing in new systems – and they also deserve to know the changes in lifestyle which switching to an alternative system will require. Consequently each category below has two ratings attached, indicating cost-effectiveness and user-friendliness.

But before continuing with the checklist, one final word: when it concerns sustainability, small is beautiful. It's very easy to solar heat a modest dwelling, for example, but exponentially more difficult to heat a mansion. Both in construction and maintenance, a small home will always consume less. And regardless of size, proper siting and design are essential in order for the technology to work.

III. Sustainability Features (continued from the previous chapter)
For cost-effectiveness (CE):
*** = highly cost-effective (no more initial cost and/or high return)
** = moderately cost-effective
* = expensive
For user-friendliness (UF):
*** = easy, rewarding
** = requires minimal input or lifestyle change
* = requires substantial energy input or lifestyle change

A. Non-toxic and Native Materials (CE✳✳✳UF✳✳✳)

Non-toxic building materials are not often grouped with sustainable building systems, but here they are at the top of the list. Why? Just ask yourself how much sense it makes to use conventional materials which increase chemical sensitivity, generate pollution during manufacture, and require energy to transport. Natural materials on the other hand are healthy, reduce pollution and energy consumption, and support the local and regional economy. They beautifully complement Archetype Design and set the tone for the appropriate technologies which follow.

B. Passive solar gain (CE✳✳✳UF✳✳✳)

Passive solar gain is no more complicated than allowing the wintertime sun to strike the south side of a building through some kind of glazing (glass or plastic). Simple, straightforward, elegant — but useless on cloudy days, so insulating window coverings and backup heat are required. There are four basic methods:

1. "Direct gain" through ordinary windows (simple, but invites glare and fading of fabrics due to ultraviolet light. Use UV-resistant glass).

2. Clerestory windows are windows placed high on a wall (sills 8'-12" above the floor) to either increase solar gain or allow light to penetrate farther into a room.

3. Trombe walls are sections of wall made of brick or masonry with glass placed over them on the exterior — this allows sun to strike the masonry and transfer slowly to the interior. The masonry actually stores the heat (acting as what we call thermal mass). The big advantage is no glare and more wall space for furnishings and wall hangings.

4. Greenhouses do double-duty as solar heat collectors and food-producing spaces. Inexpensive to build, they allow one to concentrate solar gain in relatively small areas.

    Goal for solar heating: __25% __50% __75% __100%

    Preferred method of passive gain: __windows __clerestory windows

    __trombe walls   __greenhouse

Note that proper solar design and heavy insulation will convert seamlessly to natural cooling in the summertime.

C. Active solar gain (CE*UF***)

Active solar systems use collectors mounted on the roof to absorb solar heat, which is then pumped or blown inside to heat either living space or domestic water. They are expensive, ugly, and quirky. Furthermore, it is debatable whether they ever reclaim the energy which went into their manufacture and installation. In most cases passive systems make much more sense.

D. Solar hot water (CE**UF***)

Solar water systems are cost-effective when they are skillfully worked into a design. For example, a recycled 40-gallon tank from an old electric water heater can be placed in-line under greenhouse or clerestory glazing, simply soaking up heat as the water sits in the tank. In this way water is pre-heated from 50 degrees to 90 degrees or so before entering the conventional backup water heater. For retrofits, roofmounted batch heaters cost a little more but perform quite well.

    Preferred method: __ rooftop batch heater

    __ system under clerestory or greenhouse glazing

E. Solar- and wind-generated electricity (CE**UF**)

Photovoltaic panels are those little (18"x4') panels on rooftops or ground-mounted racks which convert sunlight to 12-volt electricity. The electricity is stored in a battery bank and delivered to the house via a maze of gadgets. Usually there is a backup generator for cloudy days or system failure. Snazzy windmills are excellent additions on windy sites. Photovoltaic systems typically cost $8,000-$15,000 and are particularly attractive for sites which are far from existing power lines. Getting off the grid is a huge symbolic statement, all the more so because doing so poses significant lifestyle changes. High-voltage and energy-guzzling appliances absolutely have to be abandoned and replaced with more conservative devices: for example, propane or 12-volt refrigerators which do the job but just don't have the capacity of the conventional appliance. Lighting is used more sparingly, with compact florescents replacing incandescent lightbulbs. Most users will be particularly mindful of electrical consumption during prolonged cloudy periods. On the plus side, nothing satisfies the earth-loving heart more than knowing that one's power comes from the sun rather than from dammed rivers and coal mines.

F. Roofwater collection (CE***UF***for permacultural use)

Left to its own devices, water flowing from the roof races out of control to storm sewers, ravines or bottomland, often taking topsoil with it. A minimum goal is therefore to make sure the water stays onsite, watering trees or shrubs or even creating ponds. At the maximum, and usually due to extreme necessity, water can be conveyed to underground cisterns where it is available for either domestic use or irrigation.

> Primary use is to be:
>
> __ potable water (CE*UF*)
> __ irrigation only (CE***UF***)
> __ non-potable use (bathing, washing; CE**UF**)

G. Graywater recycling (CE*UF***)

Recycling all household water except toilet sewage is extremely sensible in arid climates. There is an initial investment for separate sewer pipes and for the second septic tank usually required by code; the water can be stored in underground cisterns at about $1/gallon in installation costs, or it can be immediately distributed to orchards, trees and shrubs. Gray water can only be used for irrigation.

H. Constructed wetlands (CE*UF***)

Once sewage water, either gray or "black", has passed through a septic tank, it may be stored in a pond which is lined with plastic sheeting, layered with gravel and sand, and planted with aquatic plants. The constructed wetlands biodigests the water and provides wonderful habitat for birds — and the overflow water is near-potable in quality. There are entire cities utilizing such systems. Expensive at $3,000-$5,000 — but a delight.

I. Composting toilet (CE**UF*)

These toilets may be site-built or purchased off-the-shelf. The advantage is in saving the water used for flushing and avoiding a septic system for the sewage; the composted by-product is of limited usefulness. Some units can be stinky, and they all require some adjustments in toilet-training. It's hard to get excited about composting toilets, but they are the best way to "go" when water is a pressing issue.

J. Drip Irrigation (CE***UF***)

Drip irrigation is absolutely wonderful: cheap, user-friendly, and water-wise. Flexible tubing placed a few inches below grade emits slow drips directly to the base of plants, and the entire system is automatically run by a time clock. Everyone should use it, period.

K. Recycling (CE***UF***)

Most of us recycle already, but the task becomes even easier with efficient collection in the kitchen and a good organizing system in the garage or enclosed area near the car or driveway. Composting, of course, is a simple and effective adjunct for anyone with gardens or landscaping.

L. Food production (CE***UF***)

Whether in an organic garden, greenhouse or orchard, growing at least part of one's own food is a wonderful way of entering into a new relationship with the land and with the food chain. For real enthusiasts, gardening is therapy, recreation and exercise rolled into one. The scope of food production can range from jars of sprouts in a corner of the kitchen to a mini-farm complete with chickens and livestock. Some systems include indoor ponds with fish or edible algae.

M. Permacultural landscape (CE***UF***)

Originating in Australia, permaculture is a comprehensive system of landuse which incorporates many of the above-listed systems. Envision a landscape where native and food-producing plants are largely sustained with roofwater, graywater, compost, and mulch; where the land is contoured to prevent erosion, windbreaks protect buildings and topsoil, and copses produce firewood and wildlife habitat. Place the house so that it is an integral part of this eco-system, and you've got permaculture.

WORKING WITH
A DESIGNER

Chapter Fifteen

The wheel symbolizes the continuously revolving laws of Nature, which are also the laws of human nature. Buddha's first sermon is referred to as the turning of the wheel of the dharma, or the setting in motion of the teachings of truth. In India the chakra is also considered to be the wheel of karma, reminding us that as we sow, so we shall reap.

Although house design provides an extraordinary arena for creative self-expression, hiring a design professional is often both necessary and desirable. It is a rare owner-builder who possesses the technical skills and confidence to go it alone. Far more commonly homeowners call in professional help right away, sometimes opting to abdicate from the entire design process. At the opposite end of the spectrum, others place such a premium on "doing their own thing" that using a designer is regarded as something of a failure. Neither extreme is likely to produce the best results. For most of us, the middle ground is the place to be — and any reader who has done the groundwork of the previous chapters will be in an excellent position to forge a fruitful relationship with an architect or designer.

The Client-Architect Relationship

With few exceptions, the most successful homes result from a dynamic relationship between the owners, who are the experts on what they want, and a designer who is an expert on how to give form to those desires.

While it is true that every architect longs for the carte-blanche commission, the fact is that most design projects thrive on a give-and-take process in which the two parties exchange energy and information, stimulating ideas which would otherwise not arise. The designer very much needs the clients to present him with fresh and unique challenges, while the owners depend upon his feedback and creativity. Exceptions do exist; moreover, there is certainly no point in hiring a professional unless one is prepared to relinquish a little control and hear what he has to say. So the decision to seek or decline help must begin with a realistic assessment of one's own needs and preferences. Only then can one move ahead to the more straightforward job of finding a designer whose skills match the work at hand.

One point cannot be over-emphasized: no matter how brilliant an architect may be, when it comes to their own happiness the owners are the absolute experts. They are the ones who must decide what they want, and then be willing to live with those decisions. In this area the architect must defer — and if he or she won't, then don't hire them.

Now let's qualify that point by saying that the best possible architect is someone with exceptional interpersonal abilities who can actually help his clients reach a deeper understanding of what will make them happy than they could have reached on their own. Traditionally, the design professional is hired for technical and aesthetic expertise only, but here we are expanding the job description by asking the architect to also have tremendous insight into people's nature and into the creative process itself. In effect, we want the architect to function in the realm of mystery as effectively as she does in her acknowledged domain of mastery.

As in any relationship, the success of the client-architect enterprise depends upon fundamentals such as recognizing each other's areas of expertise and working skillfully as a team in accordance with clear agreements. It should be obvious that the client is presenting a list of personal desires and that the first duty of the architect is to serve the client by doing everything possible to fulfill them. To this, however, Archetype Design adds some important nuances. Though the client's prior work in the realm of mystery is primarily a matter of personal vision, to the extent that one succeeds in penetrating archetypal and universal sources that vision begins to assume a transpersonal or collective aspect. Therefore only a designer who has himself made the inner journey is positioned to participate effectively in the collective aspect of the vision. The opportunity for client and professional to interact at this level is likely to create both a design and a relationship which far transcend the usual product.

Selecting the Designer or Architect

Though we have thus far been using the terms architect, designer, and design professional interchangeably, now is the time to be more precise. In most cases architects have a master's degree in architecture, have interned for one or two years under a licensed architect, and have passed the state examinations for licensing. They will usually be members if the American Institute of Architects and have "AIA" displayed on their letterhead. Architects are trained in particular to design commercial projects and to work with planners, building officials and engineers in the interests of public safety — but whether they are actually good home designers is another matter entirely. Interior designers are likewise trained and licensed, and will have "ASID" (American Society of Interior Designers) after their name. High-end clients typically gravitate to architects for reasons of status, security and credibility.

Designers, by contrast, are self-styled professionals who have no specified training but who in many states are authorized to design residential structures. While some designers are little more than glorified draftpersons, many are every bit as good as architects and have plenty of technical training or experience to back up their sense of form and function. Frequently a designer will work with a local engineer to fill in the technical gaps. Some contractors like to design as well, and are usually called design/builders. Theoretically, any one of these design professionals is capable of designing your home.

Architects, not surprisingly, will generally be the most expensive while designer/builders will be the cheapest. But neither credentials nor fees are any guarantee of performance, so the homeowner is well advised to shop carefully. The ideal professional must be able to work at several levels, which we can summarize as follows:

- technical and functional requirements
- aesthetic considerations
- quality and cost control
- sustainability issues
- managing the design/build process
- people skills
- the creative process
- vision and values

Your search for the perfect designer will probably begin with word-of-mouth referrals from friends, real estate agents, or business people in related fields such as attorneys and appraisers. Since some of them will simply be touting their own friends or speakng on the basis of hearsay, you'll have to be on your toes. Remember to refer back to the qualifications we just summarized, and look for confirmation in these areas:

1. *Track record:* does the prospective designer have a list of happy clients and a proven ability to deliver on time and within budget? What do the local builders have to report?

2. *Results:* take a tour of completed projects and see if you like the flow, the function, and the looks. Allow for the fact that the owners had their own set of goals, and cut the designer some slack for the inevitable quirks.

3. *Personal skills:* is the designer able to communicate and, most important, to listen? Does he seem to have an easy relationship with the former clients you might meet on the interview tour?

4. *Willingness:* is he genuinely interested in you and your project, or does he just want to blow his own horn?

5. *Fun:* is design as much play as it is work for this person? Does he radiate the creative spark?

6. *Resources:* does he have a good grasp of the local building industry, together with a list of reputable builders with whom he has worked?

7. *Price:* are the fees affordable to you and competitive with others of comparable reputation?

8. *Business style:* is his presentation businesslike? Does he have a sample contract which is neither flimsy nor paranoid?

9. *Values and Vision:* are you on the same wavelength when it comes to underlying values, outlook, and language?

10. *Project Specifics:* how does he respond to your site and to your proposed design ideas?

11. *Gender:* it makes no difference — if we've been using the pronoun "he," that's just the limitation of language. Guys aren't necessarily tougher, and women may not be more sensitive. The best designer will bridge the gender gap.

12. *Comfort level (last, but probably most important):* business and salesmanship aside, do you trust this person? Would you choose him as a teammate? Does your body feel comfortable and at ease? If not, don't even think about it.

The Stages of Design

Your choice of designer will be formalized in a contract which specifies the construction budget, the stages of design, what drawings are produced and at which times, how much the design fee costs, what is the payment schedule, and when the design work is to be completed. There are many variations of the design contract, for which the AIA form sets the standard.

I prefer a simpler format which relies more on trust and less on armor. In this arrangement, work begins when the agreement is signed and the designer has received 10% of his fee up front. This first stage is called Schematic Design, and the goal is to arrive at a basic concept, uncluttered by detail but clear enough to satisfy the owners that the proposed siting of the house and its basic shape and size will work for them. Usually a site plan (showing the footprint of the house and garage, the driveway and parking, and all utilities), a floor plan (showing all requested rooms by size but leaving out detail like sinks, showers and stoves), and two elevations (showing the exterior profile of the house with correct proportions but omitting detail such as doors and windows) are adequate for this stage of work. Once in a while owners need a little more detail either as a visual aid or to calm their nerves — but for the most part it's appropriate to save the bulk of the details for later. When the Schematic Design is indeed found to be satisfactory by the owners, it's time to pay 30% of the fee and authorize the next stage of work — but not before reviewing the budget and confirming that the budding design is financially on track.

Design Development comes next and is essentially a question of fleshing out the Schematic Design with the thousands of details and specifications which go into a house. The original concept is certain to go through some changes as the sizes and relationships of rooms begin to come alive — just how much the design changes is a function both of the designer's skill and the owners' ability to visualize and be decisive. This is a time for trips to numerous showrooms to research appliances, doors, tile, and plumbing fixtures. This stage is detail-intensive, and it results in virtually every drawing and specification that will constitute the final set of blueprints, with the exception of technical drawings. What the owner needs to see and understand are: a revised site plan, a complete and detailed floor plan, four exterior elevations, an electrical plan, a reflected ceiling plan (if there are exposed beam ceilings), interior elevations (cabinets, built-ins, interior details), and a finish schedule. Though owners usually can't make sense of them, the designer should also have prepared a foundation plan, section drawings and framing plans which show how the building is put together. If there's to be an engineering review, the results should be incorporated now. Once again, the budget should be reviewed, perhaps with the aid of a contractor who is quite current on building costs.

When all of this is complete and satisfactory, it's time for another progress payment and the authorization to commence the final stage of the Construction Documents. This final package has to provide all the information required for contractor's bid, building permit, and actual construction. It will include, in finished form, all the blueprints listed above as well as a booklet of narrative specifications with lists of materials, finishes, and performance standards for the construction. It's a monumental array of information, and when it's completed your designer will well deserve his final 30%.

In most high-end projects or houses built for out-of-towners, the architect is retained to oversee the entire construction, beginning with the selection of contractor and ending with approval of the completed project together with the final payment. While the cost of such extended services may be prohibitive for the average homebuilder, it usually pays to keep the designer around at least through the negotiations with the contractor. It's insurance that you're getting a fair value for your money, and you'll appreciate his assistance even more if you have to find ways to pare down the project cost at the last minute.

Working with a Designer

The ease of working with a design professional is a direct function of the skill with which you selected him in the first place and of how well you have done your homework. Once the contract is signed, you won't have much control over how well he or she is going to do their job — and you'll have none at all over their personality. But you can influence the process immensely by your ongoing ability to communicate your vision and your desires, and by your skill at building a working relationship.

The rhythm of the design process goes like this: the owners begin by presenting a set of problems and some possible solutions, the designer responds with drawings and explanations, and the owners offer positive and negative feedback. Then the loop goes around again — each time at successively more specific and detailed levels, until at last a level of comprehensive detail is reached which completely reflects and integrates the original, overarching vision. It's a relatively simple process, and a good architect knows how to both structure and pace the work. At best, it's like Michelangelo releasing the sculpture from the stone. There are just a few pointers which can make an enormous difference:

1. The more fun the better, like kids with Legos or dollhouses, the happiest homebuilders relate to the project more as play than as work. Coffee breaks, lunches, and downtime with your designer go a long way towards keeping the creative spark alive.

2. When standing firm for your wishes or giving negative feedback, always remember that even the most accomodating person wants to have their efforts recognized and appreciated. By all means assert yourself, but mind the relationship at the same time.

3. Do your homework well. Whether in the area of mystery or mastery, it's your clarity about who you are and what you want to accomplish which frees the architect to work towards the same goal.

4. Refrain from consulting other experts, or at least be extremely discreet. Nothing undermines an architect's enthusiasm like being second-guessed. It's much better to choose the right person at the start, stick with the decision, and don't look back.

5. Homebuilding is truly a joint venture, co-designed by you and the architect. Neither party should ever lose sight of the collective nature of the work, nor fail to respect their partners for their contribution.

6. It's a rare case where things go awry and the design contract has to be terminated. But there should be a clause in the contract protecting both parties: the designer should be paid for any phase of work which you have authorized, even if you terminate before that phase is completed. And the owner should reserve the right to terminate at any time, retaining possession of all the work in progress.

Some readers may confront the special challenge of having to convey an unusual vision to an architect or designer who is relatively unprepared to understand it, let alone bring the vision into being. Fortunately, Archetype Design is grounded in universal principles which have been demonstrated over the centuries, most obviously in nature-based and sacred architecture. It should not be too hard for an architect to get the basic idea, especially if he is willing to read this book. Nevertheless, there may remain a gap between your vision and his, in which case it will be up to you to provide the bridge by being especially aware and communicative. The mandalas, narratives, and schematics which you prepared early on will now be invaluable.

Needless to say, designers can benefit from reading these pages and applying the same principles to their side of the bargain. The client-architect relationship is very definitely a two-way street, and the professional will do well to temper the notorious architect's ego in favor of the Journey — for when the very process of design becomes one of transformation and healing, the result is bound to be a happy one for all.

COUPLES AT WORK

Chapter Sixteen

The hand held up in greeting signifies kindness and harmlessness, while the spiral refers to the Journey as the central fact of our existence. The hand print is thus a signature of our essential human nature.

Couples entering the design/build process face a daunting set of real-life challenges which demand real-life solutions. The best and deepest design work is useless if a couple fails to survive the building process, and thus it is essential to support the transpersonal approach by improving the skills of communication, planning and decision-making. Stress management is a desirable part of the program, and it will be greatly facilitated by being able to anticipate the most common bumps on the road of homebuilding.

The heat of the construction process, as we have remarked, is a terrible time to begin working on relationships. No sooner is the ground broken than the project moves from the realm of hopes and dreams to a harsher reality of time and money. The atmosphere can be charged with urgency and fear as the financial implications of every decision, every delay, and every mistake loom large. Time equals money for the contractor, and his need for quick decision-making seldom allows for the creative and relaxed process which characterized the planning stage. Relationships are sorely stressed under such conditions. Yet for the building to be charged with the energy of creativity and wholeness, our goal is to remain just as open, communicative and creative as we were when the dream began. The unambiguous lesson, drawn from countless projects, is to be prepared well in advance.

The work of preparing for a design/build project can be organized in four categories:

1. Vision - *what we want the house to be*
2. Goals - *what we want to accomplish in the context of time and money*
3. Decision-making - *the who's and how's of making decisions*
4. Communicating - *speaking, listening, and resolving differences*

1. Vision

Though it is obvious to envision what we want our house to be, it is rather less common to articulate who *we* want to be as we dwell in that house. Yet, as it is often said of a happy relationship that "I like who I am when I'm with that person," we could say the same about one's home. The house only exists to promote happiness and to serve either oneself, a couple, or a family — and thus to be clear about personal vision is to define what the house should be. This, quite pointedly, is most of what we did in Part One of this book.

A clear vision — and in the case of couples, a well-communicated one — provides the essential foundation for the project of design and construction. This does not mean that a couple must agree on everything. Two people must, of course, have "enough in common" to hold them together, but it is even more important to acknowledge and celebrate differences. The likelihood is that if differences are frankly and creatively accomodated as a house is built, they can be equally successfully resolved once the home is occupied.

2. Goals

Goals refer to the process of anchoring vision in the realities of time and money. Though this could (and ultimately will) be extended to include all the details of design, the important early step is to frame the project in terms of short- and longterm planning: when we want to build the house, how much money we want to spend on it, and how the project fits into the overall plan for family, career, finances, and personal goals. Such planning can be facilitated by moving through the following checklist.

1. *Family:* if there are or will be children in the picture, develop a timeline for the house in terms of how it will serve the needs of a growing family and what is the probable outcome when the children leave home.

2. *Careers:* develop a realistic outlook for the career paths of both partners, paying close attention to the issues of job stability, mobility, and the financial future. Compare this timeline with that of family, and compare the financial outlook with the financing of the house to see if all three are compatible.

Finances:
a. *Estimated cost of home.* Begin by estimating the size of the future home (refer to the wish list in Chapter 14) and its cost. Estimating requires considerable research and should include consultations with designers or builders who are in touch with current building costs. Always provide for a contingency fund of 10% of the project cost — this is your back-up and a critical anxiety-reducer.

b. *Financing.* Determine how much money may have to be borrowed, and confirm with a prospective bank or mortgage company that you qualify for the loan. List all related financing costs: appraisals, title insurance, filing fees, closing costs, and points. Find out how long the financing process takes and add 25% for contingency — financing *always* takes longer than promised.

c. *Competing cash demands.* List any expenses such as car payments, tuition, or childrearing which may compete with housebuilding or mortgage payments for your cash resources.

d. *Sale of your old house.* Get your house appraised, find a good and honest realtor, and develop a realistic timeline and financial expectation for the sale.

Timeline: develop a timeline for the following steps:
a. *Design and planning.* Three or four months is usually adequate for designing a house, depending on its intricacy and your own ability to make decisions. Allow enough time to avoid having to make snap decisions, but keep the timetable crisp enough to generate momentum and energy.

b. *Financing* usually takes 4-6 weeks and requires a finished set of blueprints at the time of application for the appraisal.

c. *Contract bidding and negotiations* require a month or longer.

b. *Construction.* Allow six months for the construction of an average house of 1,500-2,000 square feet (here you can consult prospective builders). Expect a two-week process of moving in, discovering mistakes, and working with the builder to get the wrinkles ironed out.

5. *Absences:* list any wishes you have for vacations, sabbaticals, travels, studies, or retreats which might overlap the design / build timeline. Give each a date and possible duration, and see if they are compatible with both the timeline, decision-making and financial demands of housebuilding.

By the time these five steps are completed, your planning for the house should be well-grounded in the realities of time and money. Congratulations – you have just dealt with half of the stressful obstacles over which couples and individuals come to grief! We can now go on to the key interpersonal skills of decision-making and communication.

3. Decision-making

There is no fixed way for a couple to make decisions. Each couple is different and brings to the design process a different style of working. In the end, all that matters is that a couple is happy with a decision and with each other. However, here are a few guidelines which have proven helpful in the past:

1. Whenever possible, make decisions together.

2. Identify any area of design where one partner has a special interest (eg. the primary cook and his/her kitchen). These are the most appropriate places to defer to one's partner – provided that one's own interests and input are not ignored.

3. When one partner is an expert (a professional designer, for example) special care has to be taken to include the less expert partner so that he or she can go through the design process at their own speed and eventually arrive at the same conclusion. Staying in pace with each other in this way will empower both parties and head off the subtle resentment which otherwise may arise.

4. Never make a unilateral decision, especially in an area where your partner would want to participate. Nothing undermines trust faster than one person feeling that their partner has acted behind their back.

5. Avoid giving in or compromising too quickly as you work out decisions. Maintain a balance between assertiveness and acquiescence. As a rule, it's best to speak up and maintain a dialogue, even when confronted with an impasse. Often it just takes time and patience for the solution to a design problem to present itself.

6. Don't hesitate to seek help from design professionals – their advice can often resolve a discussion quickly.

7. Remember: *it's only a house.* Step back from time to time and maintain a balanced perspective. The world won't stop turning over the choice of kitchen faucet. There are times when it really is best to let go.

8. But remember: *it's a house!* To the extent that we are designing our selves, there are times when it's best to assert yourself and explore a design issue as deeply and thoroughly as possible. It's never good to kid yourself into saying that an issue doesn't matter when in fact it really does.

9. Whenever possible, make a decision, stick to it, and don't look back. Obsessing on what-might-have-been robs the present moment of energy and subtly undermines the partnership, particularly if one partner begins to blame the other. You are both going to make plenty of mistakes – so simply acknowledge them, learn whatever lesson is available, and then let go.

These are by no means rigid guidelines – there are countless variations on these themes, and a couple should certainly take what's useful and discard the rest. The important thing is to convert unspoken decision-making "rules" into conscious agreements, and to establish a system which takes advantage of individual skills while still allowing each partner the level of participation they desire.

4. Communicating

The ability to communicate well is the single most important skill to bring to the design process. Even the best design idea is useless if it can't be successfully communicated. Vision, goals, and decision-making all depend upon one's ability to communicate – and so does the work of financing and building the house. This is true for individuals, and for couples it's doubly true.

The basic sequence for successful communication goes as follows:

1. First do your personal work so that you are free to communicate something which is truthful, to the point, and stripped of extraneous emotional charge.

2. Pick a favorable time when your partner is prepared to listen. Don't bring up a touchy issue when your mate is rushing off to work or exhausted after a long day. Bedtime is without a doubt the least skillful moment to bring up construction issues.

3. Speak from the first person and let your concerns be clearly and directly expressed (eg., "I want the dining room window to be large because". . .)

4. Always be prepared to listen. Listening doesn't just mean hearing the words coming from someone's mouth. It has to take in the timing, the body language, the subtleties of speech and gesture. Above all, listen until you can hear your partner's heart – the degree of passion which is present, or attachment, or joy, or fear.

5. Avoid interrupting, and don't be too hasty to reply — a snappy rejoinder is often taken to be a counterassault. Rather, take a breath and create a sense of spaciousness; and when you do reply, begin with a reassurance that you heard what your partner said. Sometimes, when communication has been particularly rocky, it's wise to recap what you just heard virtually word-for-word. Once your partner knows that he has been heard, only then will he be ready to listen to you. Often the simple fact of being heard resolves everything instantly.

6. When you say you are going to do something, be sure to do it. Words must be expressed in appropriate actions or they will have no power. For the same reason, when you make a commitment or ask for one, be sure to specify a timeline.

There are several additional tips to further effective communication:

1. When listening, ground yourself with the breath. Listen with your whole body. Remember that the feeling center is in the body, not the mind.

2. Fast-paced conversation is great for excited brainstorming or for the passionate sharing of new ideas. But for problem-solving, especially when emotions run high, resort to a slower pace with more calm and space for reflection.

3. Don't be too quick to cite experts, authorities, and the opinions of all your well-meaning friends on a given matter. First state your own views and preferences in the first person, then hear your partner's views. Offer an authoritative view gently, if at all — if you come on like a freight train, you'll only create a crash. It's great if you have mutually agreed-upon sources for advice, but it's even better to develop your own inner authority.

4. Coming together in a ritual way can effectively take communication to a more caring level, connecting a couple to the mythic and archetypal sources of both relationship and design work. A working session preceded by meditation, invocation or prayer sets an intention which will bear a different fruit than a random exchange. Equally important during the stress of building is to take time off and create intimate and romantic moments in which to nurture the relationship.

5. Listening is by far the most powerful part of communication. It is very common that obstinate clinging to a design feature has nothing to do with design, but is actually rooted in an unconscious emotional need. Such a need can never be solved by design details — one simply has to listen attentively and let the difficulty resolve itself at the level where it actually exists. It's amazing how our clinging can instantly dissipate when we feel that we have been listened to and heard.

Avoiding the Bumps on the Road

From purchasing the building site to moving in the furniture, the course of a building project is studded with potentially stressful developments, all of which are much more manageable if we are prepared for them in advance. The first of these stressors are themes which are more or less constant throughout the project:

1. The shift from dream to reality can come when the building site is purchased, when designing begins, or when ground is broken — or it can resurface months later while selecting paint or tile. It can be painful to have to reckon with the realities of time and money, and for many people it involves deep anxiety and a real aversion to making any important decisions at all. The solution is to do whatever research is necessary to feel in control, to get good advice, and to make the decision-making a proactive and enjoyable process. It's perfectly possible to function effectively and dream the house into being at the same time.

2. In designing, beware of getting ahead of oneself — there is a temptation to jump prematurely at solutions rather than remaining centered and sticking patiently with the process. Staying grounded in the breath and in body-awareness is a great technique — you'll sense right away when you've lost your center and are beginning to get frantic.

3. Similarly, be careful to stay in pace with your partner. It's not at all bad for one partner to become more enthusiastic than the other, but care is required to ensure that one person doesn't feel left out of the process.

4. Differing skills have to be utilized carefully. One partner may be much better able to visualize, while another may have a better business sense. One may have an eye for color while the other is good with proportion. Actually this is desirable, for every team needs good players. The biggest challenge to the team approach is when one person is a design professional – sometimes there's no way around deferring to the more skilled partner, but to be successful it takes extra sensitivity to incorporate the other's needs. One must also be prepared for the inevitable times when one partner is busy elsewhere and simply can't participate, leaving the other with the entire responsibility of making decisions and reporting on progress.

Finally we come to the step-by-step process of designing and building:

1. *Developing the wish list* (see Chapter 14) is an initial step in organizing your desires and goals. This is the first test of a couple's ability to form a mutual goal, and it requires careful communication, a little give-and-take, and some adjustment to the high stakes of building.

2. *Setting a budget* complements the wish list. This is the first point where dreams can collide brutally with reality – the big advantage is that it's only a paper collision. Here is your last chance to get grounded in financial reality before any checks are written or contracts are signed. Although it may be painful to let go of cherished dreams you simply can't afford, the benefit of setting realistic goals now is that you won't have to suffer rude awakenings later on.

7. *Selection of the architect or designer,* as we know from Chapter Fifteen, is the moment when you invite an outsider onto the team. This is also a financial commitment, and it represents another increment in letting go of dreaming and accepting the transition towards construction.

8. *The design process* should be given enough time to be unhurried, while not dragging on so long that momentum and energy fail to build. In most cases 3-4 months is adequate. The budget should be constantly reviewed to avoid nasty surprises later on.

9. *Selection of contractor* is a huge decision. It should be made on the basis of skills (which should match your project), cost (matching your budget), and personality (which should complement your own). All three criteria are essential, but personality is the factor most overlooked: consider that the contractor is also part of your team and that you'll want him as a longterm resource months or years after the house is completed. Every communication should be designed to build a good working relationship. Much the same applies to the construction crew whose sweat, vibes, and even blood go into the house — a few hellos and deliveries of coffee and donuts go a long way towards constructing a happy house.

   The construction contract itself should be thorough without being paranoid, and it must be based on complete plans and specifications so that details don't slip through the cracks. In most cases your architect will help find the builder and guide you through the contract negotiations. One simple device can save you lots of stress later on: request the contractor to give you a decision-making timetable so that you can anticipate the months of decisions without urgency on your part or his.

10. *Groundbreaking* is an occasion for celebration. Traditionally it is preceded by a ceremony of blessing, which is a wonderful way of bringing your team and your friends into the vision of creativity and transformation. On a practical level, be forewarned that a house always looks small when laid out on the ground with strings or lime — don't worry, because like Alice in Wonderland the house will change size several times along the way!

11. It is as the walls go up that the building first begins to reveal itself. It's an exciting time. Views are framed, rooms are defined, and the basic flow of the house can be felt. However, much is left to the imagination without a roof to complete the enclosure, and some homebuilders feel confused at this juncture. If the planning was thorough there won't be much to change, but a careful walkthrough is a good idea just in case. This is the last opportunity to make changes with relative ease.

12. *The raising of the roof* is both a symbolic and actual turning point, often marked with ceremony. Exterior masses are defined, interiors have been created, and now proportions are complete. Cause for celebration.

13. *Rough-in* of the plumbing and electrical systems comes next. This is not an inspiring sight, yet it's one which calls for a watchful eye, particularly to make sure that electrical devices are placed where you want them. Many small changes are usually made at this time, and it will help if your builder or designer walks you through the entire house, marking locations for lights, switches and receptacles. Have your wits about you on this visit, because it's very hard to think clearly amidst a jungle of wires and busy crews.

14. *The selection of finishes* begins much earlier than most people think. For example, the choice between a tile or a wood floor might have to be made early on so that concrete slabs can be poured at the right level. Again, a schedule from the contractor allows you to make decisions in a relaxed way. Finishing is the part of a project where enthusiasm tends to wreak havoc on the budget — the spread of costs is huge when it comes to finishes, and it's easy to get carried away and forget the financial implications of faucets, tile, light fixtures, and plaster. Be prepared to balance desires with budget, and to let go of finishes which you simply can't afford. The installation of finishes is an ongoing process requiring countless decisions: for example, once you have chosen a tile someone still has to deal with color of grout, width of grout lines, and the entire layout.

15. *Change orders* come up in every project despite the best and most complete plans. Your contract should have a clause stating that any changes or additions will be written up, assigned a lump sum price by the builder, and approved by you and/or the architect in writing before the work is performed. In practice, however, it is frequently necessary to make a change on the spot — while the backhoe is onsite, for example, or while the electrician is placing lights — in which case the paperwork will have to follow later. This requires a certain level of trust between you and the builder, which presumably began when you negotiated the contract and has continued to grow in the course of construction. Similarly, contracts are often signed on the strength of allowances for unspecified items, and months later the actual costs may vary. There are a thousand ways to "pad" an upcharge, and trust in your builder is the best assurance that the charge is appropriate.

16. *Contract disputes* over quality or cost do arise, but are easily resolved when the trust level is high and communication is good. Most experienced builders carry unpleasant memories of past losses and are very careful to avoid conflict by keeping current on client approvals and paperwork. So once again, your choice of builder proves to be very important.

17. *Quality control* is an ongoing issue in housebuilding. Most state laws specify that work shall be performed "in a workmanlike manner," but this term is so vague as to be useless. Some contracts contain language specifying "exceptional workmanship," or require architect approval of certain work. It is important to select an honest builder whose past results match your expectations, and if in addition your contractor takes pride in his work, all is likely to go well. On your part, what is required is balance: your job is to be assertive about your expectations, yet you must also communicate skillfully and maintain the integrity of the team.

18. The *"punchlist"* is the final inventory of incomplete or faulty items when the house is substantially complete or ready for occupancy. Even on the best of jobs there are punchlist items such as backordered hardware, scratched woodwork, or sticky window cranks. Your job is to do a complete walkthrough and draw up the punchlist. Sometimes a sum is assigned to the list and withheld from the final payment until the defects are remedied. If the builder has proven to be shaky in his follow-through, this retainage is his incentive to get the work done promptly. In most states he is obliged to warrant the entire house for one year after completion, though really good builders will usually fix defects for a much longer time.

Like any other enormous undertaking, a building project is much less intimidating if it is reduced to its many component parts. If the tips in this chapter are taken to heart, there simply is no reason that homebuilding should tear a couple apart, provided that they have a healthy relationship to begin with. On the contrary: given good preparation and effective personal skills, homebuilding is a rare opportunity for building and strengthening a relationship, from the foundation on up.

IN CONCLUSION: MYSTERY AND MASTERY

Chapter Seventeen

Found in cultures as disparate as the Celtic and the Tibetan, the endless knot weds the idea of the labyrinth with the image of a seamless and eternal life process. Frequently the knot takes the form of an ouroboros, emphasizing the regenerative aspect of death-and-rebirth.

Twenty-five years ago, arriving in Taos as a young man ready to settle down and grow a family, I had the good fortune of spending many hours with Little Joe Gomez of Taos Pueblo. As near as I could tell, Joe (or Grandpa, as we used to call him) had the secrets of the universe mischievously packed inside his five-foot frame, yet he had the rare and special gift of never letting on that he was into anything exceptional. Well, almost never — once in a while he'd give us a glimpse into a reality which would blow our youthful minds, and then, of course, he'd pretend that nothing had happened. One day Joe and I were sitting around at his place smoking the handrolled cigarette which was the obligatory warm-up to any meaningful conversation, when he led me out of the hogan to a stand of juniper trees a few yards away. Standing in the morning sun, Joe got right to the point and announced, "The trouble with white man is, he doesn't know his Mother." This was spoken utterly without rancor, but rather with the softness of the clouds which were forming over the distant sacred peak. I found myself dissolving into the milky, cataract-glazed depths of the old man's eyes as his words sank in. "You see that tree?" Joe said. I nodded. "It's not just a tree," he finished. At that moment, something big happened to me — it was one of those times when the mind stops and you feel like you're slipping between worlds into an ultimate reality which seems all the more real for the fact that you can't say a damn thing about it. Just like that, Joe took me smack into the Mystery, catalyzing an unfolding which has continued for all these years.

Grandpa was one of those beings who was a walking, talking presence of empty and loving space. Being with him was a glorious timeout from the everyday mind — all you had to do was enter his orbit, and wonderful things would happen. It was as if we young folks were all compressed computer files, and he was the program which instantly unzipped us. Then he'd kind of sit back and enjoy the show as we all proceeded to expand or explode in our different ways. No matter what we had to report, his invariable reply was to say, "That's good."

Although Little Joe could have been a big, successful guru, instead he was content being a master of his own simple life, living on his appointed corner of the earth and fulfilling the duties of a Taos Pueblo Indian and grandfather of forty. Joe's sense of place was evident under every fingernail, and he lived in a world in which the very earth was composed of the bones of his ancestors. His dwelling was a funky little log hogan which his young friends built for him. It had a dirt floor, a wood stove, no electricity, and water was carried by bucket from the irrigation ditch to be heated over the fire. In a land where water is sacred, Joe thought that toilets were virtual sacrilege – an outhouse was just fine with him. But Joe also loved to go to town, visit friends and have a good time. At parties he'd be dancing Indian-style, lifting one foot and then the other just as at pueblo round dances. In his last year the old man was concerned about the changing weather patterns, and so he ran in the ceremonial foot race which is the Taos way of enjoining the Sun to continue its journey. It was to be his last gift to the people and to the land, because afterwards he fell ill and never recovered.

There aren't too many like Little Joe walking the earth these days, though there sure are plenty of pretenders. It's risky to tell his story here, because it might give the impression that we should all race to rip out our toilets and live on dirt floors – but that's not the point. The point, really, is much simpler. It is, in Joe's words, to know the Mother and then just let things happen according to her rules.

This is what Archetype Design is all about – to penetrate the Mystery, and to enjoy the cascade of healing and creative energies which begin to issue forth. Some of these events will simply heal us and expand our sense of self, while others will take architectural form and direct us to sustainable ways of living with family, community and the environment. It's also about having the discipline and courage to change in step with an emerging vision, which may in fact require us to let go of comfortable but destructive ways of living. It's about placing ourselves on a continuum with a collective past which stretches back through our evolution to the most primal laws of nature – and it includes preserving that continuum for our children and grandchildren. There is a new myth to be created which is far more sublime than the timeworn American Dream, and this is the work at hand as we enter a new millennium. As householders we can build homes which surpass our former dreams even as we grow beyond our former sense of self. And if we are architects, we can move ever deeper into the Mystery at the same time that our mastery of materials and techniques helps others bring their vision into being.

HOLOTROPIC BREATHWORK™

Appendix A

Like the double-helix of our own DNA, the twin serpents of good and evil spiral gracefully around a central world-axis which is crowned with the wings of Mercury, the alchemical agent of healing. Only when both the dark and the light forces within us are recognized and brought into balance can healing take place.

H olotropic Breathwork is a technique developed by Stanislav Grof, M.D. and Christina Grof to create non-ordinary states of consciousness for purposes of systematic self-exploration, personal transformation, and healing. It was a breathwork experience (descibed in Chapter Five) which catalyzed both the concept of Archetype Design and the writing of this book.

Holotropic Breathwork offers much the same possibilities as shamanic journey, psychedelics, ecstatic drumming and dancing, austerities, psychoactive plants and dreamwork. For anyone interested in delving deeper into the psyche in search of creativity and transformation, the breathwork can provide the vehicle — quickly, simply, and without using any substances or dealing with the trappings so often associated with esoteric techniques.

Unlike the general expectation, Holotropic Breathwork is not a yoga-like technique of breathing in a prescribed way. Rather, it is as much an attitude or intention as it is a technique. A group comes together for the purpose of making the inner journey, a pair of facilitators tends to the surroundings and provides assistance, and a combination of pre-recorded music, enhanced breathing, and a supportive atmosphere release the psyche to go where it will. While some participants breathe quite forcefully, others breathe very gently, yet enjoy the same results. In other words, letting go is the key, and the breath serves as the vehicle.

"Holotropic" literally means "moving towards wholeness," which accurately describes the most mysterious aspect of the process — for in session after session, the psyche reliably generates an experience which goes in a healing and wholesome direction. As in any healing, the journey can entail considerable pain, but it is never more painful or challenging than one is prepared to successfully undergo. So remarkable is this self-guiding faculty of the psyche that breathworkers speak of surrendering to the Inner Healer. Each one of us has an Inner Healer — but it turns out that it's actually the same Inner Healer operating in everyone. So when a dozen or so people circle up to work together, a subtle but extremely powerful field of energy is collectively generated. Most participants report an intensity or depth of experience which can seldom be approximated either alone or in groups of two or three.

A Holotropic workshop typically takes all day, preceded by an orientation meeting the previous evening. Everyone works in pairs: in the morning one partner "breathes" while the other "sits," and in the afternoon the roles are reversed. The sitter's job is to give the breather continuous and one-pointed attention, and to be available for any need which might arise (kleenex, a trip to the bathroom, or perhaps a held hand). Many sitters report experiences which are unexpectedly profound, affording a rare degree of connectedness with another human being and, by extension, with the entire group. Conversely, breathers appreciate that the presence of the protective and caring sitter is an integral part of allowing the psyche to fly absolutely free during the session.

The range of experience made available by the breathwork, already described in previous chapters, can be as "ordinary" as the release of blocked physical or emotional energy or as extraordinary as archetypal and mystical visions. Lying on a mat with eyes closed, the breather journeys for 2-3 hours while a taped music program, played quite loudly, stimulates and supports the journey. Though the work is primarily a solo venture, the facilitators go about the room late in the session offering a particular type of bodywork to help release any energy which might have become hung up in the body. The facilitators, though not necessarily therapists, are trained to help the participants process any physical or emotional events which might arise. Afterwards, the breather goes to an adjacent room and draws a mandala as the first means of recording and communicating the experience in a non-verbal way. At the end of the day the entire group circles up to share their journeys, display the mandalas, and continue the process of integrating and communicating the day's experience.

Grof Transpersonal Training is the organization which trains and certifies Holotropic Breathwork facilitators, of which there are presently over one thousand worldwide. For listings of faciltators and workshops in your area call GTT at 415-383-8779 or visit the website at holotropic.com.

SEVEN CHAKRA BREATH MEDITATION

Appendix B

Seven is the number associated with spirituality, and the seven chakras of the subtle body represent the energy centers which the kundalini energy activates and opens as it rises to completion at the crown chakra. Asian temples commonly feature seven tiers or pagodas.

In the yoga tradition there are seven principal levels of awareness which are localized in the body as seven centers, called chakras. Chakra means wheel, and hence the chakras are frequently visualized as spinning wheels or discs, each with distinct colors and details. The mandala at the beginning of this chapter shows their locations.

Different energies and levels of awareness are associated with each chakra. The first chakra is the seat of kundalini, or primal energy, and is our connection with the natural world and the lowerworld. The second chakra is the level of sexual energy, which is also the fundamental energy of creativity. Chakra three, just below the navel, is the center of power, of will, and of transformation. The fourth is the heart center, the seat of compassion and the beginning of truly spiritual work. The fifth chakra is located at the throat and is associated with self-expression, truthfulness, right speech and right action. The sixth chakra, low in the center of the forehead, is sometimes called the third eye and pertains to self-knowledge, intuition and psychic powers. The crown chakra is the seventh and last, and represents wisdom and wholeness.

Each of the chakras carries a particular energy which is essential for full human development. Although the progression superficially appears to be a hierarchy, in fact the chakras form a system in which each chakra depends upon the others. The "lowest" is the seat of kundalini or *shakti*, which is the primal power of the universe resident in our body — without her we go nowhere. The sexual power in the second chakra manifests as the creation of new forms. The third chakra provides the will to reach our goals, the fire in the belly being the energy of transformation. So our meditation recognizes this interdependence and seeks to generate a strong flow of energy between the chakras as well as within each one.

Taking your seat as in vipassana meditation, begin by grounding yourself for a minute or two in the rising and falling of the breath. When you feel sufficiently present, briefly scan the chakras one by one, beginning at the bottom. Notice any sensation of energy or heat at each chakra - you may, if you wish, visualize each chakra as a stationary or whirling disc of appropriate color. Though at first these sensations might be faint or even undetectable, just go on through the sequence and use each chakra as an object of your attention.

The next step is to add energy through a forceful and rapid breath. Sometimes called the "fire breath," this is a rapid (about thirty reps in ten seconds) but shallow breath created by quick bellows-like movements of the abdomen. This breath generates a lot of energy – in fact, one must be careful to pull back if the feeling of light-headedness becomes too strong. The fire breath is not appropriate in the case of heart ailments or high blood pressure, in which case a gentler breath will suffice. A little experimentation will lead to a rate and duration of the breath which is comfortable for you.

Now focus on one chakra at a time, breathing for twenty or thirty seconds as if directly into the chakra. At the end of that time inhale and hold the breath for a few seconds, then exhale and breathe normally, allowing the awareness to float on the chakra. Notice any energy or heat present there, which with practice will increase as a consequence of the breath. Then go on to the next chakras, all the way up to the crown and back down to the base of the spine. Do this as many times as you like, noticing the sensations in the chakras, flows of energy between them, and perhaps meditating on the characteristics of each. Be prepared to work with any feelings or images which seem to be connected to a particular chakra – this work is very likely to reveal wounds or energy blocks which call for healing. Sometimes an affirmation is useful: for example, "may my sexual and creative energy flow freely," or "may my heart be open." At the end of the meditation, sit quietly for a few moments and sense the whole body with its energy flows and vibrating centers.

This meditation can be taken to great depths, using different breaths to explore the intricacies of each chakra and the flow of kundalini through the body. For our purposes, however, this practice as described is quite adequate for generating energy, increasing body awareness and stimulating spiritual growth. For example, we may find that the energy in a particular chakra is very weak and needs to be developed through extra breathwork — perhaps complemented by work on the corresponding areas of your life. Remember that both the number seven and the seven chakras are archetypes, and so we have an opportunity to directly increase awareness at an archetypal level. The symbols of serpent, ouroboros, shakti, shiva, the wheel, and the caduceus may also feed into this work through visualization, journey, or dream.

THE ASTROLOGICAL HOUSE

Appendix C

The zodiac is a mandala, or cosmogram, which depicts the universal laws connecting psyche and cosmos. The wheel, the bindu, the spiral, and the sun are all present in this rendering. The number twelve is the perfect division of time according to the combined energies of three (the divine) and four (nature).

A strology is an ancient archetypal system which dates at least as far back as the city states of Mesopotamia which we described in Chapter Two. Not for nothing were the sages of those early cities engaged in contemplation of the heavens from the tops of ziggurats and pyramids. The first sciences of mankind — mathematics and astronomy/astrology — were fundamentally concerned with coming into harmony with the gods and the forces of nature. Hence the zodiac as we know it can be viewed as a cosmogram, or mandala, which encodes the intricate patterns of nature as they exist both within us and in the cosmos. The study of astrology, then, is simply a way of penetrating those patterns so that we may take our place in the fabric of the universe in a more conscious and creative way.

For anyone pursuing a path of creativity and transformation, astrology bestows two benefits. First, without having to develop an especially deep understanding, one can quickly enhance one's intuitive ability to respond to life's constantly changing rhythms of expansion and contraction, creativity and receptivity. But for anyone prepared to explore astrology more thoroughly, the investigation can open a way to understand with greater precision our array of individual gifts and difficulties, and to appreciate how they tend to modulate and develop against the backdrop of a lawfully changing universe. Of particular interest to Archetype Design is the possibility of predicting and better utilizing periods of heightened creativity, of determining what kind of work might be favored during a given time (eg. structural vs. visionary), and of identifying individual predispositions in matters of aesthetics and structure which have a direct bearing on house design.

It must be said right away that astrology is an enormously complex art, leaving any hope of a comprehensive investigation far beyond the scope of this book. Hence the present goal is to simply highlight certain dynamics which have particular significance to design. What follows, then, are three themes which illustrate how astrological understanding can enhance the creative and transformational potential of our work.

Saturn and the Principle of Structure

When we speak of the planets in astrology, we are actually referring to the archetypal energies which they symbolize. Venus, to pick a familiar example, symbolizes love, beauty and relationship, while Mars has to do with raw energy and assertiveness. While Venus is a feminine quality and Mars is masculine, they are not gender-specific — both men and women have complementary drives to connect yet assert, to love yet survive.

The planet Saturn is central to architecture, because it is the archetype of structure manifesting in many forms and at many levels. Psychologically, structure might involve intellectual constructs and patterns as well as modes of spatial perception. Culturally, structure could refer to the taboos and often unwritten codes of social conventions, while behaviorally it could reflect the shape of our habits and lifestyle. In addition, Saturn is the planet which "rules" the physical structures of architecture, which by now we understand to be both a reflection and a shaper of psychic structures. Saturn is all about being grounded in physical reality — in architectural terms, it manifests as form and function, as organization in matters of decision-making, timeline and budget.

Archetypally, Saturn/structure refers to limits or laws, both natural and manmade. Although in the popular view Saturn is often dreaded as the archetypal grim reaper, in fact the many positive qualities of the planet deserve to be credited. The I Ching perfectly describes the contribution of Saturn in the hexagram entitled Limitation:

Water over lake: the image of limitation.
thus the superior man
Creates number and measure
And examines the nature of virtue and correct conduct.

We are told in Richard Wilhelm's commentary that the individual life achieves significance only through discrimination and the setting of limits — otherwise one's life would only dissolve into the boundless. In just the same way, architecture creates structure by limiting boundless space in a meaningful fashion. In perfect parallel, the action of structure (Saturn) in the psyche confers order and meaning as well. Here again we encounter the correlation between house and self and the possibility of creating physical structures which will structure psychic reality in a favorable way. So far, so good — but when we deal with structure there are some obstacles we should try to avoid. For like everything else, Saturn has a shadow side: excessively applied, structure can be a harsh and constricting obstruction to the flow of spirit.

Of course, structure or limitation only has meaning in contrast to its polar opposite, which is the quality of expansive growth symbolized by the planet Jupiter. Everyone loves this planet because it lights up everything it touches with optimism, happiness, success, and growth. But Jupiter, too, has its shadow: left unchecked, the energy of expansion can become inflated, grandiose, and ultimately unsustainable. Jupiter can exhibit the quality of growth-for-growth's sake — in which case Saturn is needed to provide the corrective force which curbs Jupiter, shapes its growth, and offers meaningful precision and proportion. So in Jupiter and Saturn we see one of life's primary dynamics: expansion and contraction, freedom and restraint.

Most of us suffer from some degree of helplessness regarding the Jupiter-Saturn dynamic. At times we might feel like passengers on a cosmic pendulum, alternating between the intoxicating freedom of expansion and what the I Ching calls the "galling limitation" of structure. Moods may swing uncontrollably. One moment we may feel tight, depressed and constricted, only to find ourselves on a wild shopping binge just minutes later. Rather than remaining at the mercy of such forces, astrology offers us the option of better understanding these cycles of experience and using them in a creative way. Nowhere is this more true then in architecture, which has so much to do with structure.

In the design process we encounter countless expressions of the theme of expansion/contraction. The size and physical features of a house are the most obvious examples, but considerations of budget, timeline, and indeed, the whole style of communication and decision-making are tremendously influenced by Saturnian and Jupiterian energies. In construction, where financial stakes are high and the results of our decisions will literally be cast in concrete, we can use all the help we can get to remain in balance. Right here is where Saturn's position in the natal chart, together with its relationship to the other planetary archetypes, can illuminate the dynamics of the psyche in a most helpful way. In the case of an especially powerful and influential Saturn, one might become aware of the need to mitigate the potential tyranny of structure, whether that influence be felt in the areas of money, home, relationship, or creative expression. Conversely, if Saturn is in a relatively weak and isolated location, and particularly if Jupiter is dominant, then it suggests the need to consciously develop a stronger Saturn (sense of structure).

The role of "inner structures" in architectural design is truly immense. For example, people with an afflicted sense of structure may tend towards buildings which are stiff, formal, and tightly compartmentalized, whereas what might actually be better for their own balance and healing would be a building with a greater degree of flow and expansiveness. The very process of design might be hampered by fixed ideas which stifle creativity, or by inhibitions which place a stranglehold on budget. The difficulty, of course, is that clients and owner-builders (and architects as well) are often blind to their own limitations and need a prod to make them venture beyond the confines of their familiar habits and perceptions. Much like wild animals which after a period of captivity may be hesitant to leave the cage, we tend to become imprisoned by the invisible structures of the psyche — which we then project into physical reality as the structures of architecture. Only when problems with structure are brought into awareness do we have any hope of breaking free.

The opposite tendency — a spontaneous leaning towards limitless expansiveness — is also a familiar phenomenon in design work. Expansive Jupiter in the absence of any mitigating influence from Saturn may incline an individual towards hilltop building sites, enormous windows, high ceilings, and big homes with open floor plans. Generally speaking we are very attracted to such personalities and the designs they create, yet upon closer inspection these buildings may suffer from lack of structure or restraint. The hilltop mansion may cross the line into being grandiose. Walls of glass may create views which are sensational but meaningless, and outsized floor plans may fail to provide the sense of proportion which we need to feel cozy and nurtured. Furthermore, such homes risk being unsustainable as expansive desires override the dictates of harmony with nature. By the same token, there may also be difficulties with cost overruns.

A review of the astrological chart can often suggest ways to balance the energies of Saturn and Jupiter — or to put it another way, to skillfully use the dynamics of expansion and contraction for growth and healing. Along the way we might benefit from many related insights. Pluto combined with Saturn, for example, correlates with strong foundations, hard work, and structures of concrete and steel. Venus and Saturn, together, suggest an elegance in the way beauty and harmony show themselves through structure. The astrological nuances of Saturn, in short, are every bit as fascinating as those of architectural structure itself.

The Positions of the Planets

The position which a planet occupies in the natal chart is a factor which strongly conditions how or where the planet's influence will be felt. The most familiar example of planetary position is the Sun sign — almost everyone who has ever glanced at magazines in the supermarket line can say something about the position of their Sun in the zodiac. But of greater interest to the designer is the circle of astrological houses (there's that *house* word again!). There are twelve of them, and they indicate the various areas of activity or spiritual work which an individual might undergo. The first house, for example, has to do with basic issues of identity or individual selfhood, while the seventh house (its polar opposite) is the area dealing with intimate relationships.

The fourth house invites our attention because it is the "house of home." It is located right at the bottom of the chart, or the nadir. The nadir corresponds to midnight (if you were born around midnight, your Sun would be here) and is consequently associated with the unconscious and with inner life. In fact, the entire bottom half of the chart is primarily concerned with internal and individual factors, while the upper half indicates areas of outward and more collective activity and expression. If an individual's planets are clustered in the bottom half of the chart, one can tell right away that this person is likely to be introverted, or at least more than usually involved with their inner world and personal values.

The fourth house has many meanings. Most obviously, it refers to one's actual house or home. For someone with no planets in the fourth house, home may be far less important than career or relationships. But depending on which planets and how many live there, home can be an absolutely central arena and vehicle for the expression of one's physical or spiritual work. Sun in the fourth house can indicate a deep identification with house and home, including the desire to build a strong and secure home and family. One's career might very well be in real estate, design, ecology, or construction. By contrast, Moon in the fourth house suggests a strong emotional connection with home and with familial and ancestral roots and values in general. Moon is concerned with the matrix of early life, especially mother and maternal energy, and its work can assume nurturing forms such as housekeeping, food preparation, and gardening.

When it comes to designing a home, astrology's fourth house is one place where we wear our hearts on our sleeves. Activity in the fourth house can instantly give indications of an individual's basic orientation towards house, family, and home life in a way which gives the designer a leg up in crafting a structure just right for the client. This will become clear as we continue through all ten planets.

Venus suggests an unusual longing for harmony and beauty both in the details of design and in home relationships. Venus at home wants to create a romantic air. Mars, on the other hand, offers the profile of someone likely to be very assertive at home — possibly with lots of energy available for home projects, but also prone to willfulness and disagreements. Venus at home is every designer's dream (if she doesn't get too self-indulgent), while Mars in the kitchen can be like a bull in a china shop — harness this energy during the design/build process, but be ready to duck!

The planet Mercury brings the energy of intellect and communication to the fourth house. This home may need a library, a well-planned computer workstation, and lots of telephones. The house may be the center for study groups of all kinds, and the owner may very well work at home. If a person writes or teaches about house and environment, we might expect Mercury to be in the fourth house. This client will be able to communicate precisely and thoroughly throughout the design process.

Uranus in the fourth house brings the element of change and innovation. This individual might prefer a contemporary home, state-of-the-art technology, or unusual and cutting-edge design features — if he had his way, he might also like to move or remodel frequently. Depend on this client for a flood of new ideas. Saturn, by contrast, would like a precise and conservative structure which obeys all the rules of design. No cost overruns on this project, but perhaps no fun either. The Jupiterian, of course, is inclined towards a large and comfortable home, a happy family, and an exuberant lifestyle. He or she is fun to design and build for, but they may have to be reminded to tone things down now and then.

Neptune, being the energy of the psychic, the spiritual, and the imaginal, creates interesting results in the fourth house. Ties with the family can be extremely intuitive and psychic, but boundaries may tend to dissolve and be weak. Being at the nadir of the chart, the fourth house is closely linked to the unconscious realms, so Neptune here suggests a very pronounced affinity for psychic phenomena, for transpersonal experiences, and for journeys into the imaginal. Such a person could be expected to have powerful encounters with archetypes and symbols of transformation. The Neptunian will be able to express herself symbolically, often preferring the language of image-and-emotion to linear communication. He or she is a natural for the process of Archetype Design and will appreciate a designer who can communicate with them at this level. Neptune, however, does not confer lots of get-the-job-done energy, and might benefit from the complementary power of Mars, Saturn, or Pluto.

Finally we come to Pluto, the outermost planet and one associated with regeneration and primal power. Sometimes Pluto is equated with shakti or Kali, and so Pluto at home can be a nearly overwhelming presence for everyone else. Volcanic transformations are likely to take place. However, Pluto is deeply grounded in the primal — she is, in fact, the immediate manifestation of the laws of nature — and so Pluto in the fourth house provides both the innate wisdom to create an environment in harmony with nature as well as the raw power needed to get it done. Like Neptune, Pluto is associated with the archetypal and the psychic realms.

The picture given by the fourth house becomes considerably expanded by examining the aspects made by other planets in the chart. (We will read about aspects and transits in just a few paragraphs). Similarly, the signs which overlap the fourth house are significant — whereas Mars in the fourth house might be assertive in a problematic way, this tendency would be softened if it were found within the harmonizing sign of Libra.

Of course, everything astrology can suggest about a design client is true for designers as well. Some architects are naturally expressive and flamboyant, while others tend to be more reserved and correct. With the aid of astrology, design professionals and clients can better "read" both themselves and each other, taking advantage of strengths and compensating for weaknesses. Ideally, all parties will be supported in taking a path of self-knowledge and balance which favors good working relationships and wonderful design.

Uranus and the Cycles of Creativity

Uranus is the planet most closely associated with innovation, awakening, and sudden change. Displays of inventiveness and creative genius might be expected from the individual with Uranus in a powerful and dynamic position in the natal chart — but what these displays might look like is another matter entirely, and is indicated by many other factors which condition change. For example, Uranus influenced by Jupiter suggests a big movement of sweeping change, whereas Uranus-Saturn would more likely result in a practical and realistic expression of originality.

However, nothing is static in the archetypal realm of astrology, any more than it is in the world of day-to-day. This is because the planets are in constant motion, creating a different set of relationships each moment — not only to each other, but to the planets of our natal charts. In astrological terms the planets in the sky are in *transit*, and the relationships or *aspects* they make to our natal chart are the transits or changing energies of the moment. So in the case of Uranus, for example, creative impulses which may have been somewhat dormant might be powerfully activated by transiting Pluto or Jupiter, and might further take artistic expression under the influence of Venus. It is this activation of Uranus by transiting planets which can result in periods of intense creativity, with the shape of the creative output being conditioned by aspects to both natal and transiting planets.

However, Uranus has a cycle of its own, quite independent of the other planets. This is because transiting Uranus can activate natal Uranus during its eighty-four year orbit of the sun. At birth, the most archetypal of awakenings, there is a conjunction. Uranus then squares itself as we reach the age of twenty-one, trines at about age twenty-eight, and reaches opposition at about forty-two. Not surprisingly, the square corresponds to the time of breaking from adolescence into adulthood, while the trine occurs along with the Saturn return, contributing to the emergence of the mature adult. A few years later transiting Uranus opposes natal Uranus at the time of mid-life crisis, often a time of both creative emergence and dramatic change. Again, the flavor or shape of the Uranian energy will be conditioned by all the other aspects in the chart. (ref. Tarnas, *Prometheus The Awakener*.)

Transiting Uranus activates any planet it touches as it circles the chart, creating a myriad of creative possibilities. If Uranus squares Saturn, one might expect a sudden and perhaps wrenching change in structure, whereas if Uranus trines Neptune, the result could be a highly creative expression of spiritual and imaginal energies.

Clearly, the nuances of just this one planet could become so complex that the casual onlooker might quickly lose interest. However, the inquiry becomes considerably more intriguing when we reflect on the advantages of being able to anticipate, and even maximize, periods of heightened creativity. Conversely, it would be helpful to spot creative blocks when they are still on the horizon. Periods of expansion and creative emergence are always bracketed by their polar opposite, and much of the art of living consists of how to deal creatively with the difficult periods in the lifecycle. When life — symbolized by the planets — blocks us in one area of work, it is usually directing us elsewhere, if only we have the eyes to see it. Astrology, quite simply, is a means of opening the eyes.

When conditions favor personal transformation and creative work, that of course is the time to jump right on it and take advantage of what appears to be a natural flow. But when the opposite conditions prevail — when the creative juices run dry and we feel stuck and utterly uninspired — then it may be best to pause and seek an alternative course of action. In a culture where we are expected to always be productive, the conventional response is to desperately jumpstart the machine by renewed effort, stimulants or sheer force of will. And indeed, circumstances often require us to hang in and simply make the best of a difficult time. But truly creative and transformational work can usually benefit from a wiser response, one which accepts the less creative times as necessary and indispensable parts of a greater creative cycle. In archetypal terms, creativity is the same as rebirth, and thus there can be no creative process without ego death and the journey through darker realms. Therefore, recognizing the low points in the creative cycle is an important step which must be supported by the willingness to descend into the depths of the psyche yet again, dying once more in order to reconnect with the life force and the archetypal sources of creativity.

Astrology is not the only way to move with the ebb and flow of the creative cycle. Taoism, for example, has a great emphasis on "remaining still until the moment of action" and staying in accord with the Way. But astrology is unique insofar as it is both a divinatory art and an archetypal system which can attune us to the very deep forces at play in both our design work and our Journey.

BIBLIOGRAPHY

Adams, Henry. *Mont-Saint-Michel & Chartres.* New York: Doubleday Anchor, 1959

Alexander, Charles. *A Pattern Language.* New York: Oxford University Press, 1977

Alexander, Charles. *A Timeless Way of Building.* New York: Oxford University Press, 1979

Arroyo. Stephen. *Astrology, Karma & Transformation.* Sebastopol, CA CRCS Publications, 1992

Artress, Lauren. *Walking A Sacred Path.* NY: Riverhead Books, 1995

Badiner, Allan ed. *Dharma Gaia.* Berkeley: Parallax Press, 1990

Baker, Paula & Elliott, Erica & Banta, John. *Prescriptions for a Healthy House.* Santa Fe: Inword Press, 1998

Barrie, Thomas. *Spiritual Path, Sacred Place: Myth, Ritual and Meaning in Architecture.* Boston: Shambhala Publications, 1996

Bovill, Carl. *Fractal Geometry in Architecture & Design.* Boston: Birkhauser, 1996

Campbell, Joseph. *The Hero With A Thousand Faces.* Princeton University Press, 1973

Campbell, Joseph. *The Mythic Dimension.* New York: Harper-Collins, 1977

Campbell, Joseph with Moyers, Bill. *The Power of Myth.* New York: Doubleday, 1988

Campbell, Joseph. *The Mythic Image.* Princeton University Press, 1974

Csikszentmihalyi, Mihaly. *Flow: The Psychology of Optimal Experience.* New York: HarperCollins, 1990

Doczi, Georgy. *The Power of Limits: Proportional Harmonies in Nature, Art, and Architecture.* Boston: Shambhala Publications, 1981

Edwards, Betty. *Drawing on the Right Side of the Brain.* New York: G.P. Putnam's Sons, 1989

Eliade, Mircea. *Shamanism, Archaic Techniques of Ecstasy.* Princeton University Press, 1974

Elger, Duane. *Voluntary Simplicity.* New York: William Morrow & Co., 1991

Feinstein, David & Krippner, Stanley. *The Mythic Path.* New York: G.P.Putnam's Sons, 1997

Fontana, David. *The Secret Language of Symbols.* San Francisco: Chronicle Books 1994

Fontana, David. *The Secret Language of Dreams.* San Francisco: Chronicle Books 1994

Gardner, William. *Creating Minds.* New York: HarperCollins 1993

Grasse, Ray. *The Waking Dream: Unlocking the Symbolic Language of Our Lives.* Wheaton, IL: Theosophical Publishing House

Grof, Stanislav. *The Holotropic Mind.* New York: HarperCollins, 1993

Grof, Stanislav. *The Adventure of Self-Discovery.* State University of New York, 1988

Grof, Stanislav. *The Cosmic Game.* State University of New York, 1998

Groves, Derham. *Feng Shui & Western Building Ceremonies.* Leicestershire, UK: Tynron Press, 1994

Hand, Robert. *Horoscope Symbols.* Atglen, PA: Schiffer Publishing, 1981

Hand, Robert. *Planets in Transit.* Atglen, PA: Whitford Press, 1976

Harman, Willis & Rheingold, Howard. *Higher Creativity.* Boston:Jeremy P. Tarcher, 1984

Harner, Michael. *The Way of the Shaman.* HarperSan Francisco, 1990

Halifax, Joan. Shaman: *The Wounded Healer.* London: Thames & Hudson, 1982

Hillman, James. Anima. *Woodstock,CT:* Spring Publications, 1985

Holger, Kalweit. *Dreamtime & Inner Space.* Boston: Shambhala, 1988

Ingerman, Sandra. *Soul Retrieval.* HarperSanFrancisco, 1991

Jung, Carl C. *Symbols of Transformation, Collected Works Vol. 5*. Princeton University Press, 1956

Jung, Carl C. *Memories, Dreams, Reflections*. New York: Vintage Books, 1965

Jung, Carl C. *The Archetypes and The Collective Unconscious, Collected Works Volume 9 Part 1*. Princeton University Press, 1990

Jung, Carl C. *Man and His Symbols*. New York: J.G. Ferguson Pub., 1964

Khanna, Madhu. *Yantra*. London: Thames & Hudson, 1979

Knapp, Bettina. *Archetype, Architecture and the Writer*. Bloomington IN: Indiana University Press, 1986

Lawlor, Robert. *Sacred Geometry*. London: Thames and Hudson, 1982

Lawlor, Anthony. *The Temple in the House: Finding The Sacred in Everyday Architecture*. New York: Tarcher/Putnam, 1994

Lawlor, Anthony. *A Home for the Soul*. New York: Clarkson Potter, 1997

Lethaby, William. *Architecture, Mysticism & Myth*. Bath, GB: Solos Press, 1990

Linn, Denise. *Sacred Space*. New York: Ballantine Books, 1995

Mollison, Bill. *Permaculture: A Designers Manual*. Australia: Tagari Publications, 1992

Marcus, Clare. *House as a Mirror of Self*. Berkeley: Conari Press, 1995

Metzner, Ralph. *The Unfolding Self*. Novato, CA: Origin Press, 1998

Moon. Beverly, ed. *Archetypal Symbolism*. Boston: Shambhala Publications, 1997

Neihardt, John. *Black Elk Speaks*. Lincoln NB: University of Nebraska Press, 1993

Nabokov, Peter & Easton, Robert. *Native American Architecture*. New York: Oxford University Press, 1989

Pearson, David. *Earth To Spirit: In Search of Natural Architecture*. San Francisco: Chronicle Books, 1995

Perry, John Weir. *Lord of The Four Quarters*. Mahwah, NJ: Paulist Press, 1991

Purce, Jill. *The Mystic Spiral*. London: Thames & Hudson, 1974

Robertson, Robin. *Beginner's Guide to Jungian Psychology*. York Beach, ME: Nicolas-Hays, Inc., 1992

Rykwert, Joseph. *On Adam's House in Paradise*. Cambridge: MIT Press, 1997

Sakoian, Frances & Acker, Louis. *The Astrologer's Handbook*. New York: HarperPerennial, 1989

Scully, Vincent. *Architecture: The Natural and the Manmade*. New York: St. Martin's Press, 1991

Sheldrake, Rupert. *A New Science of Life*. Rochester, VT: Park Street Press, 1995

Swan, James & Roberta, ed. *Dialogues With The Living Earth*. Wheaton, IL: Theosophical Publishing House, 1996

Tarnas, Richard. *Prometheus the Awakener*. Woodstock, CT: Spring Publications, 1995

Thompson, Angel. *Feng Shui*. New York: St. Martin's Press, 1996

Too, Lillian. *The Complete Illustrated Guide to Feng Shui*. Rockport, MA: Element Books, 1996

Walsh, Roger & Vaughan, Frances, ed. *Paths Beyond Ego: A Transpersonal Vision*. New York: G.P. Putnam's Sons, 1993

Walsh, Roger. *The Spirit of Shamanism*. New York: G.P. Putnam's Sons, 1990

Wilber, Ken. *A Brief History of Everything*. Boston: Shambhala Publications, 1996

Wilhelm, Richard, trans. *The I Ching*. Princeton: Princeton University Press, 1950

Wong, Eva. *Feng Shui*. Boston: Shambhala Publications, 1996

INDEX

NOTES